# America on the Brink: Military Readiness, Economic Rivalry, and Political Fragmentation

# America on the Brink: Military Readiness, Economic Rivalry, and Political Fragmentation

F.L. Hinton Jr.

Published by FRED HINTON, 2026.

AMERICA ON THE BRINK: MILITARY READINESS, ECONOMIC RIVALRY, AND POLITICAL FRAGMENTATION

**First edition. February 8, 2026.**



ISBN: 979-8233262685

Written by F.L. Hinton Jr..

# F.L. HINTON JR.

**TABLE OF CONTENTS**



## Foreword

In times of peace, nations often grow complacent. In times of crisis, they scramble to react. But the United States now finds itself in a far more dangerous place—caught in a storm where both complacency and crisis coexist. The threats are no longer on the horizon; they are here, intertwined, and multiplying. From shifting global alliances that challenge our economic dominance, to persistent terror threats that test our resolve, to bitter political divisions that erode our unity from within—America stands in a precarious moment.

America on the Brink: Military Readiness, Economic Rivalry, and Political Fragmentation is not simply a book about policy, nor is it a detached academic treatise. It is a strategic call to arms for both leaders and citizens. F.L. Hinton Jr., an entrepreneur and author with a track record of confronting the hard truths, lays bare the interconnected vulnerabilities of our military readiness, economic stability, and political cohesion. His analysis is sharp, unflinching, and grounded in both lived experience and rigorous research.

Hinton understands that the United States does not have the luxury of treating its challenges in isolation. Weakening defense capabilities affects economic confidence; market instability fuels political extremism; partisan division undermines our ability to respond to external threats. These forces do not act independently; they reinforce one another in a dangerous feedback loop.

But this is also a book about solutions. Hinton offers a blueprint for how America can rebuild strength—through revitalizing military recruitment, forging smarter economic partnerships, renewing civic responsibility, and rekindling the sense of shared purpose that once defined us. He calls for an era where public and private sectors work hand in hand, where citizens demand more from their leaders and more from themselves, and where strategic foresight replaces reactive politics.

The value of America on the Brink lies not only in its urgency but in its clarity. Hinton makes it impossible to ignore the stakes, yet equally impossible to believe that decline is inevitable. This book is a wake-up call, but also a guidepost—pointing toward a future where America can regain its footing and stand once again as a united, secure, and confident nation.

The clock is ticking. The threats are real. But so is our capacity to overcome them—if we act now.

# Chapter 1: Cracks in the Empire

"Empires do not decline because of external enemies alone; they falter when the internal will to sustain greatness frays, when confidence turns to complacency, and unity splinters into discord."
***— Niall Ferguson, Civilization: The West and the Rest***

In the sweltering summer of 1945, James "Jimmy" Sullivan, a fresh-faced Navy veteran barely out of his teens, stood steadfast on the weathered deck of a troop transport ship slicing through the vast Pacific Ocean, his gaze locked intently on the distant horizon where the shores of America beckoned like a promised land. The brutal war that had engulfed the world for years had finally drawn to a close, with the Axis powers—Nazi Germany, Imperial Japan, and Fascist Italy—crushed under the weight of Allied determination and firepower. The United States, emerging from the ashes of global conflict, stood tall as the unchallenged titan of the free world, a colossus straddling continents with its unparalleled economic might, military prowess, and ideological influence. Factories across the nation hummed with relentless activity, churning out goods that fueled both reconstruction and prosperity. Soldiers like Jimmy returned home to heroes' welcomes, complete with ticker-tape parades winding through bustling city streets, confetti raining down like celebratory snow. The American Dream, that enduring vision of opportunity, upward mobility, and personal success, seemed not just an aspiration but a tangible promise etched indelibly into the very stone of the nation's foundation. Jimmy, at the tender age of 22, harbored an unshakeable belief in his country's invincibility—a shining beacon of industrial innovation, unyielding military strength, and unwavering moral clarity that illuminated the path for the entire world.

Now, fast-forward eight decades to the year 2025, and we find Jimmy's grandson, Michael Sullivan, another dedicated veteran shaped by the rigors of service, sitting quietly in a modest coffee shop nestled in the heart of Dayton, Ohio. The aroma of freshly brewed coffee mingles with the faint hum of conversations around him as he scrolls methodically through his smartphone, absorbing the latest headlines that paint a troubling picture: escalating trade wars that disrupt global supply chains, intractable political gridlock that paralyzes decision-making in Washington, and a once-formidable military now stretched perilously thin across multiple fronts. The boundless optimism that defined the post-war era of 1945 feels like a faded photograph from a bygone time, replaced by a pervasive sense of uncertainty, anxiety, and deep-seated division that permeates every layer of society. Michael, reflecting on his own experiences and the legacy passed down through generations, finds himself pondering a profound and unsettling question: How on earth did we arrive at this precarious juncture? What forces, both visible and insidious, have eroded the foundations of American supremacy?

This chapter undertakes a detailed examination of America's meteoric rise to unparalleled global dominance in the immediate aftermath of World War II, while meticulously identifying the early warning signs—the subtle yet insidious cracks in what was once an impenetrable empire. These vulnerabilities manifest in various forms: creeping economic stagnation that saps vitality from the nation's productive core, military overstretch that drains resources and morale, and intensifying domestic polarization that fractures the social fabric and undermines collective purpose. These fissures, which began as barely noticeable hairline cracks in the grand edifice of American power, have over time deepened and widened into profound structural weaknesses, posing existential challenges to the nation's enduring ability to lead on the world stage. However, as we will argue throughout this narrative,

America's decline is far from an inevitable fate sealed by history's inexorable march. By delving deeply into the origins and nature of these cracks, we can illuminate a viable path toward renewal, reinvigoration, and resurgence. This story holds particular resonance for veterans like Michael, who bear the personal weight of a nation in flux, for students eager to grasp the historical context that shapes contemporary realities, and for policymakers entrusted with the solemn duty of steering the ship of state away from the rocks and toward calmer waters.

### The Post-War Pinnacle

The United States emerged from the cataclysmic crucible of World War II not merely as a victor but as the undisputed preeminent power on the global stage, a position of dominance that reshaped the international order for generations. By the pivotal year of 1945, the U.S. economy had ballooned to account for nearly 50% of the entire world's gross domestic product (GDP), a staggering figure that underscored its role as the engine of global recovery and growth. American factories, which had been repurposed during the war to produce everything from Sherman tanks and B-29 bombers to ammunition and supplies on an unprecedented scale, transitioned seamlessly into peacetime production, flooding markets with consumer goods that symbolized abundance and progress. The U.S. dollar, fortified by the innovative Bretton Woods system established in 1944, ascended to the status of the world's reserve currency, providing a stable foundation for international trade and finance that bolstered American influence far beyond its borders. The U.S. Navy, with its formidable fleet of aircraft carriers and battleships, patrolled the seven seas with unchallenged authority, ensuring open sea lanes and projecting power across oceans. Military bases dotted the globe, from the tropical islands of the Pacific to the heart of Europe, serving as outposts of American resolve. Culturally, the U.S. exported its soft power through iconic symbols—Hollywood films that captivated audiences worldwide with tales of heroism and romance, the infectious rhythms of jazz music that echoed in cafes from Paris to Tokyo, and everyday products like Coca-Cola that became synonymous with modernity and freedom. This era epitomized American exceptionalism, a deeply held conviction that the nation's blend of economic vitality, military superiority, and democratic ideals rendered it not just superior but uniquely destined to lead humanity toward a brighter future.

The empirical data from this period paints a vivid and compelling picture of this ascendancy. In 1945, the nominal U.S. GDP stood at an impressive $228 billion, towering over the Soviet Union's comparatively modest $90 billion and utterly dwarfing China's economy, which had been ravaged by years of invasion and civil strife, amounting to a mere $20 billion. The U.S. military, having swelled to a peak strength of over 12 million personnel during the height of the conflict, remained unmatched in size, training, and technological sophistication, while its exclusive possession of nuclear weapons—demonstrated dramatically in Hiroshima and Nagasaki—ensured absolute strategic superiority that deterred potential adversaries. On the diplomatic front, the United States took the helm in forging key institutions that would define the

post-war world: the United Nations, established to promote peace and cooperation among nations; NATO, a military alliance that bound Western Europe in collective defense against Soviet expansionism; and the Marshall Plan, a visionary aid program that funneled billions of dollars into rebuilding war-torn Europe, not only fostering economic recovery but also securing long-term allies and markets for American goods. For veterans like Jimmy Sullivan, who had witnessed the horrors of combat firsthand—from the island-hopping campaigns in the Pacific to the liberation of concentration camps in Europe—this was an era infused with profound pride. America was no longer just a sovereign nation; it had evolved into a global mission, a force for good committed to spreading liberty, prosperity, and stability across a weary world.

Yet, even amidst this golden age of triumph and exuberance, the seeds of future challenges were quietly sown, taking root in the fertile soil of victory. The United States voluntarily assumed the mantle of global policeman, pledging to defend allies scattered across the map—from the bustling ports of Japan in East Asia to the industrial heartlands of West Germany in Europe. This expansive commitment, while noble in intent, inevitably stretched finite resources thin and established lofty expectations that would prove increasingly difficult to sustain as the decades unfolded.

Domestically, the euphoric post-war economic boom, characterized by suburban expansion, the baby boom, and rising consumerism, masked underlying inequalities that simmered beneath the surface. Racial segregation persisted in the South and beyond, denying African Americans and other minorities full participation in the American Dream; gender disparities confined women largely to domestic roles despite their wartime contributions in factories and offices; and labor tensions, fueled by strikes and union demands, hinted at class divides that could erupt into broader social unrest. The intoxicating confidence of 1945, born from hard-won victories and apparent invincibility, inadvertently bred a dangerous complacency—a widespread assumption that American dominance was not a fragile achievement to be nurtured, but an eternal state of affairs ordained by destiny. This mindset, while uplifting in the short term, would later contribute to a reluctance to adapt to emerging threats and internal shifts, allowing those initial seeds of vulnerability to germinate into more formidable problems.

**Economic Stagnation: The Slow Erosion**

By the dawn of the 21st century, the once-robust economic foundations that underpinned American power had begun to exhibit signs of wobbling instability, a gradual erosion that threatened the very pillars of national strength. The United States' commanding share of global GDP, which had peaked at nearly half the world's total output in the immediate post-war years, had steadily diminished to approximately 24% by 2025, as reported by the authoritative projections of the International Monetary Fund (IMF). Meanwhile, China, emerging from decades of isolation and reform, had surged forward with remarkable speed, boasting a

GDP of $18.3 trillion in purchasing power parity (PPP)-adjusted terms by the same year. This ascent enabled China not only to close the gap but also to surpass the U.S. in critical areas, such as manufacturing output and overall export volume, reshaping the global economic landscape in profound ways. To illustrate this dramatic shift in fortunes, consider the following detailed table, which tracks the evolution of GDP shares over key historical milestones:

| Year | U.S. GDP Share (% of Global) | China GDP Share (% of Global) |
|---|---|---|
| 1945 | 49.8% | 1.5% |
| 1970 | 36.1% | 4.1% |
| 2000 | 30.7% | 7.2% |
| 2025 | 24.3% | 18.9% |

Source: IMF World Economic Outlook, 2025 (projected).

This decline is not merely a statistical anomaly but a reflection of deep-seated structural issues that have plagued the American economy for decades. The process of deindustrialization, which accelerated in the 1970s amid globalization and technological change, systematically hollowed out once-thriving manufacturing hubs such as Detroit, Michigan—famed for its automotive industry—and Pittsburgh, Pennsylvania, the steel capital of the world. Factories shuttered, jobs migrated overseas to lower-cost labor markets, and entire communities were left grappling with unemployment, urban decay, and social dislocation. By 2025,

the U.S. manufacturing sector had shrunk dramatically, employing just 8% of the national workforce, a sharp drop from the 24% it represented in 1960, according to comprehensive data from the Bureau of Labor Statistics. Concurrently, trade deficits exploded to unsustainable levels, with the United States importing a staggering

$3.1 trillion more in goods and services than it exported in 2024 alone, a significant portion of that imbalance attributable to trade with China, which flooded markets with affordable electronics, textiles, and machinery. Adding to these woes, the national debt ballooned to an astronomical $34 trillion by 2025, equivalent to 120% of GDP, severely constraining the government's fiscal flexibility and limiting investments in infrastructure, education, and research that could spur long-term growth.

For individuals like Michael Sullivan, these abstract economic figures translate into tangible, everyday struggles that erode quality of life and hope for the future. As the owner of a small machining business in Ohio's Rust Belt, Michael constantly battles competition from cheaper Chinese imports that undercut his prices and squeeze profit margins. His employees, many of whom are fellow veterans or blue-collar workers, contend with stagnant wages that fail to keep pace with inflation—real median household income has inched up at a meager annual rate of just 0.8% since the turn of the millennium. The post-war promise of widespread prosperity, where hard work guaranteed a comfortable middle-class existence complete with home ownership, college education for children, and secure retirement, now feels like a relic of a distant past. Automation, driven by advances in robotics and artificial intelligence, further exacerbates job losses, displacing workers in sectors from assembly lines to logistics. Globalization, while benefiting consumers with lower prices, has widened income inequality, with the top 1% capturing a disproportionate share of economic gains. Rising costs for essentials—housing, healthcare, and education—outstrip income growth, forcing families to make difficult choices and fostering a sense of economic insecurity.

Policymakers are confronted with a complex dilemma: aggressive reinvestment in domestic industry through subsidies, tariffs, or infrastructure projects risks igniting inflationary pressures that could destabilize the economy, while neglecting these issues altogether cedes even more ground to rising rivals like China, potentially accelerating America's relative decline. This economic

stagnation, therefore, is not just a matter of numbers on a spreadsheet but a profound challenge to the social contract that has long defined the American way of life.

**Military Overstretch: The Cost of Empire**

The U.S. military, historically the unyielding backbone of global order and a symbol of American resolve, now confronts its own array of deepening cracks that compromise its effectiveness and sustainability. Following World War II, the United States constructed and maintained an expansive global network of over 700 military bases, strategically positioned from the humid jungles of Okinawa in Japan to the sprawling airfields of Ramstein in Germany. This vast infrastructure, designed to deter aggression and project power instantaneously, comes at an enormous annual cost—estimated at $150 billion in 2025—placing immense strain on national budgets at a time when domestic priorities such as healthcare, education, and infrastructure demand urgent attention. The concept of military overstretch, a term popularized by the eminent historian Paul Kennedy in his seminal work "The Rise and Fall of the Great Powers," aptly describes the burdensome toll of sustaining such far-flung commitments, where resources are diluted across too many theaters, leading to fatigue, inefficiency, and vulnerability. The protracted wars in Iraq and Afghanistan serve as stark case studies of these limits; initiated in the early 2000s with ostensibly clear objectives of regime change and counterterrorism, these conflicts devolved into protracted quagmires characterized by insurgencies, nation-building failures, and shifting alliances. The human and financial costs were staggering: over $6 trillion expended, more than 7,000 American lives lost, and countless more wounded physically or psychologically, all of which eroded public support and sowed seeds of war-weariness among the populace.

Recruitment challenges represent another alarming red flag signaling deeper systemic issues within the armed forces. In 2024, the U.S. Army fell short of its enlistment targets by a significant margin, securing only 55,000 new recruits against a goal of 70,000—a shortfall of 15,000 that highlights recruitment difficulties across branches. The underlying reasons are multifaceted and intertwined with broader societal trends: a robust civilian economy offers attractive job opportunities that diminish the appeal of military service; demographic shifts mean fewer eligible young people due to obesity, criminal records, or educational deficiencies; and perhaps most critically, Generation Z's growing skepticism toward traditional institutions has dampened enthusiasm for enlistment. According to a 2024 Gallup poll, only 43% of young Americans express trust in the military, a notable decline from previous generations influenced by factors like perceived endless wars, scandals, and cultural shifts. Michael Sullivan, drawing from his own experiences as a former Army sergeant who deployed multiple times to the Middle East, fondly recalls the unbreakable camaraderie and sense of purpose that bonded his unit through adversity. However, he observes with concern that today's recruits often face outdated equipment, inadequate training budgets, and missions clouded by ambiguity, which further erode morale and retention rates.

The Pentagon's fiscal allocations underscore these challenges. The 2025 defense budget, totaling a colossal $850 billion, remains the largest in the world by far, yet its distribution reveals inefficiencies: approximately 60% is allocated to personnel costs, including salaries, benefits, and pensions, alongside routine maintenance of aging hardware, leaving scant resources for critical modernization efforts. In contrast, emerging rivals such as China have adopted a more focused approach to military spending, with an estimated $300 billion budget in 2025 directed disproportionately toward cutting-edge technologies like hypersonic missiles capable of evading traditional defenses, artificial intelligence-integrated command systems, unmanned drones for surveillance and combat, and advanced cyber warfare capabilities that threaten digital infrastructure. The U.S. Navy, once the undisputed master of the seas with fleets that dominated every ocean, now fields a fleet of 290 deployable ships in 2025, lagging behind China's rapidly expanding navy, which boasts over 340 vessels, including aircraft carriers and submarines optimized for regional dominance in the South China Sea. For veterans like Michael, these disparities signal a military apparatus stretched to its breaking point, struggling to maintain readiness amid competing demands. For policymakers, this reality demands urgent and comprehensive reform: streamlining bureaucracy, prioritizing innovation, enhancing alliances to share burdens, and redefining strategic priorities to avoid overcommitment. Without such adaptations, the cost of empire risks becoming an unsustainable weight that accelerates decline rather than bolsters security.

**Domestic Division: The Enemy Within**

Perhaps the most profound and insidious crack afflicting America's empire is the rampant domestic polarization that has transformed a once-unified nation into a patchwork of ideological battlegrounds. The sense of national unity that characterized 1945, forged in the fires of shared sacrifice during World War II—where Americans from all walks of life rallied behind a common cause, from factory workers producing war materiel to families enduring rationing, has fractured irreparably into opposing camps defined by partisanship, cultural clashes, and mutual distrust. A comprehensive 2024 survey conducted by the Pew Research Center revealed a startling statistic: 80% of Americans now perceive the opposing political party not merely as a rival with differing views, but as an existential "threat to the nation's well-

being," a dramatic increase from the 60% reported in 2000. This escalation is amplified exponentially by the pervasive influence of social media platforms, where sophisticated algorithms curate

content to reinforce existing beliefs, creating insulated echo chambers that deepen divisions and stifle dialogue. In Michael Sullivan's own family, this national rift manifests on a personal level: his sister, a committed progressive living in the tech-savvy environs of Seattle, Washington, advocates for social justice reforms and environmental policies, while his uncle, a staunch conservative rooted in the rural farmlands of Ohio, clings to traditional values and economic protectionism. Their once-close relationship has deteriorated to the point where they haven't spoken meaningfully since the contentious 2024 presidential election, a microcosm of the broader societal fragmentation.

This entrenched polarization extends beyond personal relationships to paralyze the machinery of governance, rendering effective policymaking an increasingly rare occurrence. In 2024, the U.S. Congress managed to pass only 27 pieces of significant legislation, a paltry output compared to the 70 bills enacted in 1994 during a period of relative bipartisanship. Initiatives that could enjoy broad support—such as comprehensive infrastructure upgrades to modernize roads, bridges, and broadband access, or targeted military reforms to address recruitment shortfalls and technological lags—frequently stall in the quagmire of partisan rancor, with each side prioritizing political point-scoring over pragmatic solutions. Public trust in core institutions has plummeted to historic lows: a 2024 Gallup poll indicated that only 16% of Americans express confidence in the federal government to act in their best interests, while trust in the media stands at a dismal 31%, eroded by accusations of bias and sensationalism from all sides. For students studying American history and politics, this dynamic provides a critical framework for understanding the roots of contemporary gridlock, tracing it back to evolving cultural norms, economic disparities, and the rise of identity politics. For policymakers navigating this treacherous terrain, it represents a full-blown governance crisis that hampers responses to pressing challenges, from climate change to economic inequality.

The cultural ramifications of this division are equally stark and far-reaching, undermining the shared narratives that once bound Americans together in a common identity. In the post-war era, unifying figures like the trusted news anchor Walter Cronkite delivered impartial reporting that fostered a collective understanding of events, while landmark achievements such as the Apollo 11 Moon landing in 1969 inspired national pride and a sense of limitless possibility. By 2025, however, these cohesive elements have been supplanted by contentious debates over the nation's history and values: the removal of Confederate statues sparks protests and counter-protests, school curricula on topics like critical race theory or gender education ignite parental backlash and legal battles, and even public health measures, such as vaccine mandates during pandemics, become flashpoints for ideological warfare. These conflicts fuel resentment and alienation, eroding the social cohesion necessary for a functioning democracy.

Veterans like Michael find themselves caught in this crossfire, proud of their service to a country they love but increasingly alienated by a society that appears to prioritize partisan division over shared duty and sacrifice. The result is a nation where common ground seems elusive, and the "enemy within" poses a greater threat to stability than any external adversary.

**The Veteran's Lens: A Narrative of Change**

Michael Sullivan's personal journey serves as a poignant mirror

reflecting the broader trajectory of America's evolution from post-war pinnacle to contemporary crossroads. Enlisting in the U.S. Army in 2015 at the age of 20, Michael was deeply inspired by the vivid tales of heroism and valor recounted by his grandfather Jimmy, whose WWII experiences—from surviving kamikaze attacks in the Pacific to witnessing the raising of the flag on Iwo Jima—painted a picture of unadulterated glory and purpose. Yet, Michael's own deployments to the volatile theaters of the Middle East unveiled a starkly different reality: missions plagued by unclear objectives that shifted with political winds, pervasive local distrust toward American forces seen as occupiers rather than liberators, and a military apparatus stretched across an array of fronts from counter-ISIS operations in Syria to stabilizing efforts in Afghanistan. The camaraderie among troops remained a source of strength, but the toll of improvised explosive devices (IEDs), ambushes, and the psychological strain of asymmetric warfare left indelible scars.

Upon returning to civilian life, Michael encountered a homeland profoundly transformed and fractured. His small business in Dayton, specializing in custom parts for local manufacturers, grapples daily with supply chain disruptions exacerbated by global trade tensions and pandemics, forcing delays and increased costs that threaten viability. His community, once a tight-knit enclave of working-class solidarity, is now riven by divisions over issues ranging from vaccine policies and public health mandates to voting integrity and electoral reforms, with neighbors eyeing each other suspiciously across ideological lines. The unbridled optimism that Jimmy embodied upon his return in 1945—envisioning a future of endless opportunity and national greatness—has faded into a faint, nostalgic echo for Michael, who perceives a nation adrift, buffeted by internal storms and external pressures. This sense of disorientation is compounded by personal challenges: navigating the bureaucracy of veterans' benefits, coping with post-traumatic stress, and witnessing friends struggle with unemployment or addiction in a society that offers lip service to "supporting the troops" but falls short in substantive aid.

Yet, amid this narrative of change and challenge, Michael's story also radiates glimmers of hope and resilience. He channels his experiences into positive action by volunteering at a local

veterans' center, where he mentors younger recruits transitioning to civilian life, sharing lessons on resilience, leadership, and community building. Additionally, he advocates for grassroots community projects, such as job training programs for displaced workers and bipartisan dialogues to bridge political divides at the local level. These efforts embody a steadfast belief that America possesses the inherent capacity to rebuild and renew itself—not through rose-tinted nostalgia for a mythologized past, but through deliberate, collective action grounded in pragmatism and shared values. This personal commitment resonates deeply with the overarching thesis of this book: while the signs of decline are undeniable and multifaceted, they do not predetermine a trajectory of irreversible downfall. Instead, they serve as catalysts for introspection and innovation, urging citizens from all walks of life to engage in the hard work of revitalization.

**The Path Forward**

The cracks permeating America's empire—manifested in persistent economic stagnation, debilitating military overstretch, and corrosive domestic division—are undeniable realities that demand acknowledgment and action. Since the triumphant heights of 1945, the U.S. share of global GDP has halved, reflecting a loss of economic preeminence; the military contends with widening recruitment gaps, outdated systems, and technological asymmetries relative to competitors; and societal polarization has reached levels that threaten the very fabric of national cohesion and effective governance. These challenges, compounded by global shifts such as the rise of multipolar powers and rapid technological disruption, paint a sobering portrait of a superpower at a crossroads.

Yet, it is crucial to emphasize that these vulnerabilities are not fatal flaws etched in stone, but rather surmountable obstacles that

history demonstrates America has overcome before. The nation's track record of resilience is illustrious: the New Deal programs of the 1930s rebuilt a shattered economy from the depths of the Great Depression through bold public works and social safety nets; the exigencies of the Cold War era spurred groundbreaking innovations in science, technology, and industry, from the interstate highway system to the space race; and the brief but powerful surge of unity following the terrorist attacks of September 11, 2001, showcased the potential for collective strength in the face of adversity, even if that solidarity proved fleeting. These historical precedents underscore that America thrives when it confronts crises head-on, harnessing its diversity, ingenuity, and democratic spirit to forge ahead.

For veterans like Michael Sullivan, this chapter evokes a dual sentiment: profound pride in the triumphs of the past, from the beaches of Normandy to the innovations of Silicon Valley, and an urgent call to serve once more—whether through community involvement, political advocacy, or mentorship of the next

generation. Students, grappling with the complexities of modern geopolitics and domestic affairs, gain a robust analytical framework that roots today's crises in long-term historical shifts, encouraging critical thinking and informed citizenship.

Policymakers, bearing the weight of leadership, are reminded of the imperative for decisive reform: strategic economic reinvestment to revitalize manufacturing and innovation ecosystems, targeted military modernization to enhance efficiency and deterrence, and deliberate efforts to bridge divides through dialogue, electoral reforms, and media literacy initiatives. The subsequent chapters of this book will delve even deeper into related themes, from the ascendance of the BRICS nations (Brazil, Russia, India, China, and South Africa) as challengers to American hegemony, to strategies for internal renewal through education, technology, and civic engagement. However, the foundational lesson imparted here is unequivocal: America's empire may be cracked, marred by the wear and tear of time and trials, but it is far from broken beyond repair. True renewal commences with an unflinching confrontation of the truth, coupled with the resolve to act boldly and collectively for a revitalized future.

Diagram: U.S. vs. China GDP Share (1945–2025)

| Year | U.S. GDP Share (% of Global) | China GDP Share (% of Global) |
|---|---|---|
| 1945 | 49.8% | 1.5% |
| 1970 | 36.1% | 4.1% |
| 2000 | 30.7% | 7.2% |
| 2025 | 24.3% | 18.9% |

Source: IMF World Economic Outlook, 2025 (projected).

# Chapter 2: The BRICS Challenge

"The BRICS are not just an economic bloc; they are a signal that the American-led world order is no longer the only game in town. Their rise doesn't guarantee a new hegemon, but it does mean the

U.S. must play a tougher game—or risk being sidelined."

***— Peter Zeihan, The End of the World Is Just the Beginning***

In the vibrant month of July 2025, the sprawling Rio de Janeiro Convention Center hums with an electric atmosphere of anticipation and high-stakes diplomacy as the 17th BRICS Summit officially kicks off, drawing together a diverse array of world leaders in a display of emerging global influence. Heads of state and high-ranking representatives from the core founding members—Brazil, Russia, India, China, and South Africa—mingle alongside the newly incorporated nations: Egypt, Ethiopia, Iran, the United Arab Emirates, and Indonesia. The expansive conference halls and meeting rooms are filled to capacity, the air thick with a palpable sense of purpose and determination, as these leaders converge to articulate and advance a shared vision of a multipolar world that is progressively less dependent on the longstanding dominance of the United States and its Western allies. Brazilian President Luiz Inácio Lula da Silva, known for his charismatic leadership and advocacy for global equity, takes the stage to deliver the opening address, his voice resonating with conviction as he unveils a groundbreaking new trade pact designed to facilitate transactions in local currencies, thereby deliberately bypassing the entrenched reliance on the U.S. dollar that has long characterized international commerce. A delegate from China, representing the world's second-largest economy, follows suit by showcasing an innovative digital yuan platform, highlighting its potential to revolutionize cross-border payments with enhanced efficiency and security. Meanwhile, Russia's representative emphasizes the strategic advantages of newly viable Arctic energy routes, made accessible by the accelerating effects of climate change on polar ice caps. For the very first time in its history, this expanded BRICS bloc—now encompassing a staggering 41% of the global gross domestic product (GDP) and nearly half of the entire world's population—presents itself not merely as a loose association but as a genuinely unified and formidable force capable of reshaping the geopolitical landscape. Back in the heartland of America, veterans like Michael Sullivan, seated in his modest home in Ohio and tuning into the live coverage via international news channels, experience a profound sense of unease; this unfolding spectacle serves as a stark and sobering reminder that the post-World War II world order, meticulously shaped by the sacrifices and triumphs of his grandfather's

generation in 1945, is undergoing a seismic shift under the weight of these ascending powers.

This chapter delves deeply into the BRICS coalition as an ascendant economic and geopolitical entity, one that poses a direct and multifaceted challenge to the longstanding U.S.-led global order that has dominated international affairs for decades. We will meticulously explore the intricacies of their interconnected trade networks, their commanding control over vital natural resources, and their concerted efforts toward de-dollarization, all of which collectively undermine and threaten America's position of primacy on the world stage. Through the vivid lens of the 2025 summit in Rio de Janeiro, we witness the bloc's unity manifesting in tangible actions and initiatives, but we also uncover the underlying tensions and internal contradictions that could potentially fracture its cohesion and limit its long-term effectiveness. For policymakers in Washington and beyond, this development signals a host of strategic risks that demand immediate attention and adaptive responses; for students of international relations and history, it offers a compelling lesson in the dynamics of a truly multipolar world where power is increasingly diffused; and for veterans like Michael Sullivan, it represents a clarion call to comprehend the evolving global stakes, where old alliances may no longer suffice and new strategies are essential. Building directly upon the foundational cracks in America's empire that were identified and analyzed in Chapter 1—such as economic stagnation, military overstretch, and domestic polarization—this chapter illustrates how these vulnerabilities are now confronting a direct and organized challenge from a bloc of nations resolute in their determination to rewrite the established rules of the international system, forging pathways that prioritize their own interests and visions.

## The Rise of BRICS: From Acronym to Alliance

The BRICS coalition, which has grown from a mere economic shorthand into a robust and influential alliance, traces its origins

back to the year 2001, when Jim O'Neill, a prominent economist at the investment bank Goldman Sachs, first coined the acronym "BRIC" to encapsulate the rapidly expanding economies of Brazil, Russia, India, and China—nations he foresaw as future drivers of global growth and transformation. This conceptual framework quickly gained traction, and by 2010, South Africa had been formally invited to join, rounding out the group to form the BRICS as we initially knew it. Fast-forward to 2024, and the bloc underwent a significant expansion, welcoming Egypt, Ethiopia, Iran, the United Arab Emirates, and Indonesia into its fold, with Saudi Arabia's membership status still pending final ratification amid ongoing deliberations. This enlarged configuration, frequently referred to as BRICS+, has evolved into a demographic and economic powerhouse of unprecedented scale: it encompasses approximately 3.9 billion people, accounting for a remarkable 48%

of the global population, and boasts a combined GDP of $65 trillion when measured in purchasing power parity (PPP) terms, which equates to 41% of the world's total economic output—a figure that notably surpasses the 30% share held by the traditional G7 group of advanced economies comprising the United States, Japan, Germany, the United Kingdom, France, Italy, and Canada.

The 2025 summit in Rio de Janeiro stands as a powerful symbol of this remarkable evolution, transforming what once were relatively informal and exploratory gatherings in the early 2000s into a highly coordinated forum for substantive collaboration across trade, finance, and geopolitics. Unlike those nascent meetings focused primarily on economic discussions, the contemporary BRICS engages in comprehensive coordination that extends to policy alignment and joint initiatives. A prime example is the New Development Bank (NDB), which was established in 2015 with an initial capital base of $100 billion, dedicated to financing infrastructure and sustainable development projects in member countries without the conditionalities often imposed by Western-led institutions like the World Bank—such as requirements for market liberalization or political reforms. Complementing this is the Contingent Reserve Arrangement (CRA), another $100 billion fund designed to provide mutual support during financial crises, such as currency devaluations or balance-of-payments difficulties, thereby offering an alternative to the International Monetary Fund (IMF) and its dollar-centric mechanisms. These homegrown institutions embody a fundamental BRICS objective: to systematically reduce dependence on Western-dominated financial and developmental systems, fostering greater autonomy and resilience among emerging economies.

However, the significance of BRICS extends far beyond mere economic cooperation; it constitutes a bold political statement against the prevailing unipolar order. Influential leaders such as China's President Xi Jinping and Russia's President Vladimir Putin frequently position BRICS as a deliberate counterweight to what they perceive as U.S. hegemony, championing the concept of a "multipolar world" where power is distributed more equitably among diverse actors rather than concentrated in the hands of a single superpower. Nations like Brazil and India, while exercising caution to avoid overly confrontational anti-Western rhetoric that could jeopardize their own bilateral relations with the U.S. and Europe, nonetheless pursue enhanced influence within global governance structures, such as advocating for reforms in the United Nations Security Council or greater voting rights in international financial bodies. The inclusion of newer members like Iran and the UAE injects additional layers of complexity and strength, bringing substantial energy wealth and strategic assets that bolster the bloc's overall clout in critical sectors like oil and natural gas markets. For students delving into international affairs, this trajectory of BRICS provides a rich case study in the fluid nature of global power shifts, illustrating how economic interdependence can evolve into political solidarity. For policymakers tasked with safeguarding national interests, it serves as a stark warning of the emergence of a coordinated rival bloc capable of challenging established norms and institutions, necessitating proactive diplomatic and economic strategies to maintain relevance.

**Trade Networks: Rewiring Global Commerce**

At the heart of BRICS' formidable challenge to U.S. dominance lies its intricate and expanding trade networks, which serve as the foundational pillars for rewiring the patterns of global commerce in ways that diminish Western influence. Intra-BRICS trade volumes have surged dramatically, reaching an impressive $1.2 trillion in 2024, propelled by the complementary strengths of its members: China's unparalleled manufacturing prowess, Russia's abundant energy resources, and India's burgeoning services sector, particularly in information technology and pharmaceuticals.

Central to this integration is China's ambitious Belt and Road Initiative (BRI), a vast global infrastructure endeavor launched in 2013 that weaves together trade routes spanning continents, from state-of-the-art ports in Africa to high-speed railways crisscrossing Eurasia, facilitating seamless connectivity and economic interdependence among BRICS nations and beyond. Additionally, Russia's stewardship of the Northern Sea Route through the Arctic, increasingly navigable due to the melting of polar ice amid global warming, presents a compelling alternative to traditional Western-controlled maritime chokepoints like the Suez Canal in Egypt and the Panama Canal, potentially slashing shipping times and costs for goods moving between Europe and Asia.

To visualize this expansive web, the following textual description of a map outlines the key BRICS trade routes and resource nodes as they stand in 2025, highlighting the strategic interconnections that underpin the bloc's growing autonomy:

**BRICS Trade Routes and Resource Influence (2025)**

- China: The BRI corridors, including the overland Silk Road Economic Belt and the Maritime Silk Road, establish vital links from bustling Asian hubs to ports in Europe and Africa, enabling the efficient transport of manufactured goods, electronics, and consumer products. China maintains dominance over 80% of the world's rare earth elements, minerals indispensable for high-tech industries.

- Russia: The Arctic Sea Route, stretching from the northern port of Murmansk to Asian destinations, combined with the International North-South Transport Corridor (INSTC), connects Russian territories to Iran and India through a mix of rail, road, and sea links. Russia contributes 39% of the bloc's oil exports, leveraging its vast Siberian reserves.

- India: As a major exporter of IT services and pharmaceuticals, India utilizes key ports such as Mumbai and Chennai to facilitate intra-BRICS trade flows, particularly with the UAE and African nations, enhancing South-South economic ties.

- Brazil: Renowned for its agricultural and mineral exports, Brazil ships soybeans, beef, and iron ore from ports like Santos and Paranaguá directly to Chinese markets, with Amazonian River ports providing additional linkages for bulk commodities.

- South Africa: Serving as a supplier of gold and platinum, South Africa relies on the Durban port as a central hub for African trade, exporting minerals and resources to Asian partners within the bloc.

- New Members:

Iran: Controlling 45.9% of BRICS' proven oil reserves, Iran utilizes Persian Gulf ports like Bandar Abbas to export petroleum products to China and India, bolstering energy security.

UAE: As a global trade nexus, the UAE's Dubai ports, including the massive Jebel Ali facility, handle an annual trade volume exceeding $400 billion, serving as a pivotal distribution center for goods across the Middle East and beyond.

Egypt: With sovereignty over the Suez Canal, Egypt facilitates the passage of 12% of global trade, linking BRICS routes to European markets and reducing transit dependencies.

Ethiopia: Positioned as a Horn of Africa hub, Ethiopia accesses the sea via neighboring Djibouti ports, connecting landlocked African economies to broader BRICS networks.

Indonesia: Exporting nickel and palm oil, Indonesia's Jakarta port acts as a Southeast Asian node, channeling resources to China and India for industrial use.

Source: Adapted from IMF, World Bank, and BRICS Summit reports, 2025.

This meticulously constructed network significantly diminishes reliance on Western-dominated trade infrastructures, allowing BRICS members to circumvent potential vulnerabilities. For instance, China's substantial BRI investments in African ports

enable the bypass of U.S.-influenced chokepoints such as the Strait of Malacca, a narrow waterway critical for Asian trade but susceptible to naval blockades. Similarly, the INSTC, a 7,200-kilometer multimodal corridor developed collaboratively by Russia and Iran, dramatically reduces shipping durations from India to Europe by up to 20 days compared to traditional routes, enhancing efficiency and resilience against disruptions. By empowering BRICS nations to dictate the terms of global commerce—through preferential tariffs, joint ventures, and infrastructure ownership—these developments effectively sideline U.S. influence in key economic arteries. For veterans reflecting on historical parallels, this reconfiguration evokes memories of Cold War-era logistics battles, where control over supply lines determined strategic outcomes; for policymakers, it represents a profound strategic shift that necessitates countermeasures, such as bolstering alliances or investing in alternative routes to preserve American leverage in global trade dynamics.

**Resource Control: The Power of Commodities**

BRICS' commanding grip on critical natural resources further amplifies its geopolitical leverage, positioning the bloc as a pivotal player in the global supply of commodities essential for modern economies and technologies. Collectively, the group accounts for 39% of worldwide oil exports, 47.6% of oil production, and an astounding 45.9% of proven oil reserves, primarily attributable to the hydrocarbon-rich nations of Russia, Iran, and the UAE, whose vast fields in Siberia, the Persian Gulf, and the Arabian Peninsula fuel both domestic needs and international markets. China, meanwhile, holds a near-monopoly on rare earth minerals, controlling 80% of global supply—these elements are indispensable for the production of smartphones, electric vehicles, wind turbines, and other high-tech and green energy applications. Brazil emerges as an agricultural and mining powerhouse, supplying 40% of the world's soybeans and 20% of iron ore, commodities that underpin global food security and steel manufacturing. South Africa dominates in precious metals, providing 70% of platinum—crucial for catalytic converters and fuel cells—and 30% of gold, while Indonesia's abundant nickel reserves, vital for battery production in the burgeoning electric vehicle sector, propel the transition toward clean energy solutions.

This extensive resource dominance poses a direct challenge to U.S. economic security and strategic autonomy, as America remains heavily dependent on imports for many of these materials. In 2024, the United States imported an average of 7.5 million barrels of oil per day, with roughly 20% sourced from BRICS nations, exposing vulnerabilities to price fluctuations or supply disruptions orchestrated by the bloc. China's stranglehold on rare earths compels U.S. technology companies, from Apple to Tesla, to engage in negotiations with Beijing, often under terms that favor Chinese interests and potentially compromise intellectual property

or market access. Brazil's agricultural exports, increasingly directed toward BRICS markets like China and India, diminish the traditional reliance on U.S. grain surpluses, altering global food trade patterns and reducing American bargaining power in agricultural diplomacy. For students exploring the intersections of economics and geopolitics, this scenario vividly illustrates how control over resources can translate into soft and hard power; for military readers and veterans, it underscores the reality that supply chains are not merely logistical concerns but potential battlegrounds where disruptions can have cascading effects on national defense, industrial capacity, and economic stability, reminiscent of wartime resource shortages.

**De-Dollarization: The Financial Front**

Perhaps the most overt and immediate challenge to U.S. global dominance emanates from BRICS' aggressive pursuit of de-dollarization, a concerted effort to erode the primacy of the American currency in international finance. As of 2024, the U.S. dollar facilitated 88% of all global transactions, according to data from the Society for Worldwide Interbank Financial Telecommunication (SWIFT), enabling the United States to wield extraordinary influence through mechanisms like sanctions, which can isolate adversaries by restricting their access to dollar-denominated systems. BRICS aims to dismantle this advantage by promoting alternatives that prioritize sovereignty and multipolarity. At the 2025 Rio summit, leaders made significant strides in this direction, advancing the BRICS Pay system—a digital platform designed for seamless intra-bloc trade settlements—and encouraging the use of local currencies in bilateral deals. China's digital yuan, or e-CNY, stands as a flagship initiative, having been piloted in transactions totaling $200 billion by 2025, offering a blockchain-based alternative that promises faster, cheaper, and more secure cross-border payments without intermediary banks.

The NDB and CRA play instrumental roles in this financial reconfiguration, providing mechanisms that lessen dependence on dollar-based institutions. Since its inception in 2016, the NDB has approved funding for 96 projects amounting to $32 billion, frequently disbursed in local currencies to avoid exchange rate risks and promote monetary diversity. The CRA, functioning as a liquidity buffer, offers emergency support to members facing financial turbulence, mirroring the IMF's role but without the austerity measures often demanded by Western lenders.

Discussions and posts on social media platforms like X (formerly Twitter) frequently amplify BRICS' ambitions to "ditch the dollar" and establish a parallel financial architecture rivaling the IMF and World Bank, capturing a growing global sentiment among developing nations for alternatives that reflect their priorities. This push gained additional urgency in light of U.S. President Donald Trump's 2024 statements, where he threatened to impose

100% tariffs on BRICS nations should they proceed with abandoning the dollar, highlighting the perceived existential threat to American financial hegemony.

Nevertheless, the path to de-dollarization is fraught with substantial hurdles that temper its immediate impact. The U.S. dollar's unparalleled liquidity, backed by deep financial markets and widespread trust, remains a benchmark that BRICS currencies—such as the Chinese yuan or Russian ruble—struggle to match due to concerns over convertibility, political stability, and regulatory transparency. According to 2025 IMF estimates, intra-bloc trade conducted in local currencies constitutes only about 20% of total trade volumes, indicating that significant infrastructural and institutional developments are still required to scale up these efforts. For policymakers analyzing long-term trends, this represents a simmering risk that could erode U.S. leverage over time, necessitating diversification of reserves and alliances; for students, it provides a fascinating lesson in the intricacies of financial power dynamics, where currency dominance intertwines with geopolitical strategy and economic interdependence.

The 2025 Summit: Unity and Tensions

The narrative unfolding at the 2025 Rio summit encapsulates both the impressive unity of BRICS and the latent tensions that could undermine its aspirations. Leaders project an image of solidarity and strength: President Lula of Brazil champions the virtues of South-South cooperation, emphasizing equitable development and mutual benefit; Xi Jinping of China promotes the digital yuan as a tool for inclusive finance; and Iran's president underscores the bloc's oil leverage as a means to counter Western sanctions. Concrete actions back these pronouncements, yet beneath the surface, fault lines persist—India and China continue to grapple with longstanding border disputes in the Himalayas, which occasionally flare into diplomatic standoffs, while Brazil treads carefully to avoid alienating its lucrative trade relationships with the U.S. and Europe by tempering any overly aggressive anti-Western rhetoric. Saudi Arabia's protracted membership deliberations reflect a similar caution, as the kingdom balances the allure of BRICS with its deep-seated alliances in the West, particularly in security and energy sectors.

Despite these internal frictions, the summit's outcomes demonstrate bold ambition: an expansion of the NDB's capital by

$10 billion to fund more ambitious projects, the formalization of a BRICS+ trade agreement aimed at reducing barriers and harmonizing standards, and a collective commitment to increase local currency trade to 30% of intra-bloc exchanges by 2030.

However, the diversity of interests—India's preference for strategic neutrality, Russia's focus on circumventing sanctions imposed due to its actions in Ukraine, and the varying economic priorities of African newcomers pose risks to sustained cohesion. For veterans drawing parallels to historical alliances, this mirrors the fragile unity of Cold War blocs like the Warsaw Pact, where ideological alignment masked underlying divergences; for policymakers, it underscores the need for nuanced counter-strategies, such as exploiting these tensions through targeted diplomacy or incentives to prevent BRICS from coalescing into an unbreakable front.

**The Challenge to America**

The ascent of BRICS presents a direct and multifaceted threat to

U.S. dominance manifests across economic, geopolitical, and financial domains. Its sophisticated trade networks systematically bypass Western routes, reducing vulnerabilities to U.S. naval or economic pressures; its mastery over critical resources challenges American supply chains, potentially leading to shortages in strategic materials; and the drive toward de-dollarization undermines the financial leverage that has long enabled sanctions and global influence. With command over 41% of global GDP and key commodities, BRICS emerges as a formidable rival capable of altering the balance of power. Yet, the bloc's inherent diversity—encompassing vast cultural, political, and economic differences—imposes natural limits on its ability to achieve full unification, offering opportunities for external actors to influence outcomes.

In response, the United States must pursue a multifaceted approach: reinvesting in domestic economic capabilities to reduce dependencies, exercising diplomatic agility to strengthen alliances and exploit BRICS divisions, and modernizing military postures to address emerging threats, themes that will be explored in greater depth in subsequent chapters. For veterans like Michael Sullivan, the rise of BRICS serves as a wake-up call, reminding them that the world order forged through American leadership and sacrifice is now fiercely contested, demanding vigilance and adaptation.

Students gain invaluable insights into the mechanics of a multipolar world, where power ebbs and flows through networks of influence rather than unilateral dictate. Policymakers, meanwhile, confront a strategic imperative: to adapt proactively or risk being relegated to the sidelines in an evolving global arena. As the cracks in America's empire, detailed in Chapter 1, now encounter this coordinated challenge, the potential for renewal persists, contingent upon decisive, forward-thinking action that reaffirms U.S. resilience and innovation.

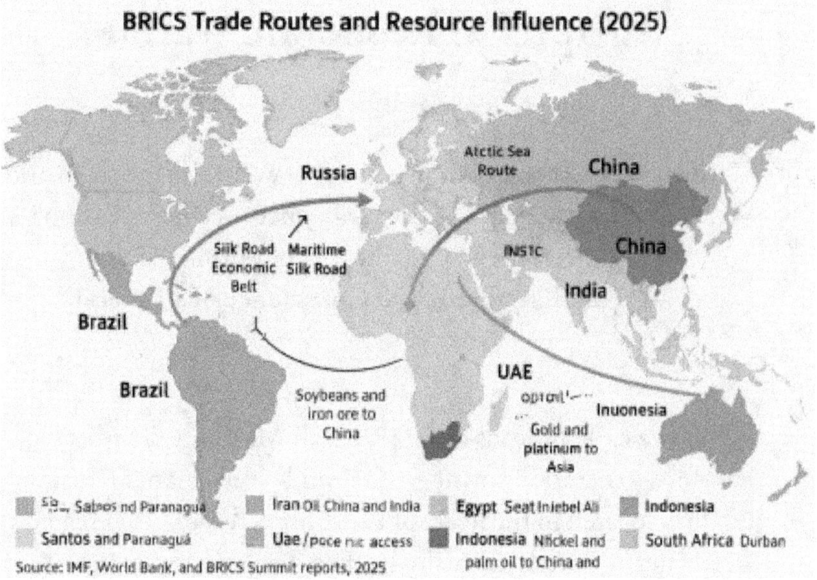
BRICS Trade Routes and Resource Influence (2025)
Russia
Atctic Sea Route
China
Silk Road Economic Belt
Maritime Silk Road
INSTC
China
India
Brazil
Brazil
UAE
Soybeans and iron ore to China
Inuonesia
Gold and platinum to Asia
Iran Oil China and India
Egypt
Indonesia
Santos and Paranaguá
Uae
Indonesia Nickel and palm oil to China and
South Africa Durban
Source: IMF, World Bank, and BRICS Summit reports, 2025

# Chapter 3: Economic Warfare

"The power to control money is the power to shape the world. When that control slips, so does influence—economies don't just compete; they wage war without firing a shot."
**— Paul Krugman, The Conscience of a Liberal**

In the early months of 2025, Sarah Martinez, a dedicated third-generation owner of a mid-sized manufacturing firm located in the heart of Pittsburgh, finds herself seated in her modestly furnished office, her eyes fixed intently on a complex spreadsheet that unmistakably signals impending trouble for her business. Her company, which has long specialized in producing high-quality steel components essential for various construction projects, has unfortunately experienced a significant loss of 20% of its orders over the course of just six months. This downturn is largely attributable to fierce competition from Chinese manufacturers, who can leverage substantially lower production costs and the innovative digital yuan payment system to undercut their prices in a highly aggressive manner. Compounding these challenges are the persistent shipping delays resulting from newly imposed U.S. tariffs, as well as the broader effects of a weakened U.S. dollar.

which have collectively rendered her exports far less competitive on the international stage. Moreover, her customers based in Southeast Asia are increasingly demanding payments in alternative currencies such as the yuan or Indian rupees, often citing the advantageous BRICS trade agreements that facilitate such

transactions. While Sarah's father successfully navigated through multiple economic recessions in the past, this current situation feels profoundly different to her—it represents a quiet, relentless form of economic war that is being waged subtly yet effectively. For Sarah personally, this struggle is deeply intimate and affects her livelihood directly; however, for the United States as a whole, it poses an existential threat to its economic stability and global standing.

This chapter delves deeply into the multifaceted aspects of economic warfare that are systematically undermining the United States' longstanding financial leverage. We will explore in detail the ongoing currency wars, the significant shifts occurring in global trade patterns, and the concerted de-dollarization efforts being spearheaded by the BRICS coalition, which includes Brazil, Russia, India, China, South Africa, and its newly added members. In particular, we will examine China's pioneering digital yuan and the emerging alternative financial systems developed by the BRICS nations, all of which are posing a direct challenge to the dominance of the U.S. dollar in international finance. Through the

personal narrative of Sarah Martinez, we gain a poignant

understanding of the human cost associated with these geopolitical and economic shifts, while simultaneously analyzing the supporting data that reveals the high strategic stakes involved. For policymakers, this discussion provides critical insights into potential strategies for countering these economic threats effectively; for students and general readers, it offers a clear and accessible clarification of the often complex and high-stakes world of global finance; and for veterans, it presents a new kind of battlefield where financial instruments like dollars, rather than traditional weapons like bullets, ultimately decide the outcomes of conflicts. Building directly upon the foundations laid in Chapter 2 regarding the broader BRICS challenge to American hegemony, this chapter illustrates how economic warfare is deepening the existing cracks in America's imperial structure, yet it also emphasizes that through strategic and proactive action, there remains a viable path toward renewal and strengthened resilience.

## The Dollar's Reign: A Fragile Throne

Since the historic year of 1944, when the Bretton Woods agreement was established during a pivotal conference that reshaped the post-World War II economic order, the U.S. dollar has served as the world's primary reserve currency, granting America an unparalleled level of financial power and influence over global affairs. According to data from SWIFT in 2024, the dollar accounts for an impressive 88% of all global transactions, while the International Monetary Fund (IMF) reports for 2025 indicate that it constitutes 59% of foreign exchange reserves held by central banks around the world. This dominant position enables the United States to borrow funds at exceptionally low interest rates, impose economic sanctions on adversarial nations with significant impact, and exert considerable influence over international trade dynamics. A prime example of this power was demonstrated in 2022 when the U.S. sanctioned Russia in response to its actions in Ukraine, resulting in the freezing of approximately

$300 billion in Russian reserves, which vividly showcased the dollar's formidable might as a tool of economic coercion. For individuals like Sarah Martinez, this system historically translated into stable and reliable contracts, as well as widespread global trust in the validity and security of her business invoices denominated in dollars.

However, despite its longstanding supremacy, the dollar's throne is increasingly shaky and vulnerable to erosion. The BRICS nations, which collectively control about 41% of the global gross domestic product (GDP) and represent 48% of the world's population, are actively pushing for viable alternatives to reduce their dependence on the U.S. dollar. As highlighted in the discussions from Chapter 2, the 2025 BRICS Summit held in Rio de Janeiro made substantial advancements in initiatives such as BRICS Pay and the promotion of trade settlements in local currencies, all aimed at diminishing reliance on the dollar. China's digital yuan, which has facilitated transactions totaling $250 billion by 2025, stands out as a particularly direct and potent challenge to the existing financial order. Similarly, since 2023, Russia and India have successfully settled around 15% of their bilateral trade using rubles and rupees, as reported by the Reserve Bank of India, further illustrating the growing momentum behind these alternative approaches. These coordinated moves not only threaten the dollar's central role in global finance but also erode the broader leverage that the United States has traditionally enjoyed through its currency's dominance.

To provide a clearer picture of this gradual decline, the table below illustrates the steady decrease in the dollar's share of global reserves over the years:

| Year | U.S. Dollar (%) | Euro (%) | Chinese Yuan (%) | Other (%) |
|---|---|---|---|---|
| 2000 | 71.1% | 18.3% | 0.0% | 10.6% |
| 2010 | 61.8% | 26.0% | 1.0% | 11.2% |
| 2020 | 59.2% | 20.5% | 2.3% | 18.0% |
| 2025 | 58.7% | 20.1% | 3.1% | 18.1% |

**Source:** IMF Currency Composition of Official Foreign Exchange Reserves, 2025 (projected)

For students studying international economics or geopolitics, this data serves as a stark illustration of the inherent fragility of financial dominance and how it can wane over time due to shifting global dynamics; for policymakers tasked with safeguarding national interests, it represents an urgent call to action to bolster and reinforce the dollar's defenses against these emerging threats.

**Currency Wars: The Digital Yuan and Beyond**

Currency wars constitute one of the most central and critical fronts in the broader landscape of economic warfare, where nations vie for influence through monetary policies and innovations rather than direct confrontation. At the forefront of this battle is China's digital yuan, officially known as the e-CNY, which is a state-controlled digital currency that was initially launched in 2020 and has since expanded to be utilized in approximately 30% of China's cross-border trade activities with fellow BRICS nations. In contrast to decentralized cryptocurrencies such as Bitcoin, which operate without central oversight and emphasize anonymity, the e-

CNY is meticulously managed by the central authorities in Beijing, enabling them to track and monitor transactions in real-time while simultaneously bypassing the traditional Western-dominated banking systems that have long been intertwined with the U.S. dollar. By the year 2025, this digital currency will have processed over 1 billion individual transactions, amounting to a staggering $250 billion in total value, according to official reports from the People's Bank of China. This remarkable growth allows China to extend an attractive dollar-free alternative to its BRICS partners, which is particularly appealing to countries like Iran that have faced stringent U.S. sanctions and are seeking ways to circumvent such restrictions.

The impact of this shift is acutely felt by business owners like Sarah Martinez in her day-to-day operations. Her clients in Southeast Asia, who were once content and even preferred to conduct payments in U.S. dollars due to their familiarity and perceived stability, are now increasingly opting for the e-CNY because of its notably lower transaction costs and its inherent immunity to potential disruptions caused by U.S.-imposed sanctions. A specific instance that highlights this challenge occurred in 2024 when a promising deal with a Malaysian firm ultimately fell through because Sarah's company lacked the necessary infrastructure to accept and process payments in yuan, leaving her unable to meet the client's evolving preferences.

Adding to this complexity is the BRICS Pay system, which was

officially launched in 2024 and has since integrated various national currencies within the bloc, successfully processing around $100 billion in intra-bloc trade by 2025. This system is further complemented by Russia's Mir payment network and India's Unified Payments Interface (UPI) platform, together forming a robust and parallel financial ecosystem that operates independently of the dollar-centric frameworks.

These concerted efforts are significantly weakening the effectiveness of U.S. sanctions as a foreign policy tool. For instance, when the United States targeted Russia's energy sector with sanctions in 2022, Moscow adeptly pivoted by shifting a substantial portion of its trade settlements to yuan and rupees, thereby mitigating the economic losses that might have otherwise been more severe. Estimates from the Center for Strategic and International Studies (CSIS) suggest that approximately 20% of global trade now bypasses systems based on the U.S. dollar, marking a notable increase from just 10% in 2015. For veterans who may have experienced the economic blockades and pressures of the Cold War era, this modern scenario evokes familiar parallels in how economic measures can be wielded as weapons; for policymakers currently in positions of authority, it underscores the pressing need to develop new and innovative tools to preserve and maintain American influence in an increasingly multipolar financial world.

**Trade Shifts: Rewriting the Rules**

The ongoing shifts in global trade patterns are exacerbating

America's existing vulnerabilities, creating imbalances that go beyond mere economic statistics and touch on strategic national security concerns. In 2024, the U.S. trade deficit ballooned to an alarming $1.1 trillion, with China alone responsible for a disproportionate $400 billion of that figure, as documented by the

U.S. Census Bureau. This persistent imbalance is symptomatic of a much deeper and more structural transformation: the BRICS nations are deliberately redirecting their trade flows away from traditional U.S.-centric routes toward more intra-bloc and

alternative partnerships. A key driver of this change is China's ambitious Belt and Road Initiative (BRI), which has seen investments totaling $1 trillion across more than 150 countries worldwide, funding the construction of ports, railways, and other infrastructure projects that prioritize access to BRICS markets and reduce dependence on Western-controlled trade corridors. For example, the China-Pakistan Economic Corridor has become a vital artery for commerce, facilitating the annual movement of $62 billion worth of goods and services, effectively bypassing routes that might be subject to U.S. influence or disruptions.

These global trade shifts are having a direct and detrimental impact on businesses like Sarah's manufacturing firm. The tariffs that were imposed in 2024 as a measure to counter what was perceived

Chinese dumping practices have inadvertently raised her input costs by about 15%, making it harder for her to maintain competitive pricing. At the same time, persistent delays at U.S. ports, which have been clogged by ongoing supply chain disruptions stemming from various global events, resulted in the loss of a lucrative $2 million contract that could have provided much-needed revenue. In contrast, the BRICS trade agreements, such as the comprehensive pact signed during the 2025 Rio Summit, have successfully lowered tariffs among member nations, thereby enhancing the competitiveness of their internal markets and fostering stronger economic ties. Notable examples include

Brazil's robust soybean exports to China, which reached a value of

$50 billion in 2024, and India's thriving IT services trade within the BRICS framework, amounting to $100 billion, both of which demonstrate the emergence of a self-sustaining economic bloc that operates with increasing autonomy.

The United States finds itself struggling to mount an effective response to these developments. Protectionist policies, such as the proposed 100% tariffs on goods from BRICS nations that were floated in X posts by former President Trump in 2024, carry the risk of escalating into full-blown trade wars without necessarily addressing the underlying root causes of America's trade disadvantages. According to reports from the World Trade Organization, there has been a 10% decline in the U.S. share of global exports since the year 2000, while exports from BRICS countries have experienced a substantial growth of 25% over the same period. For general readers who may not delve deeply into economic reports, this trend helps explain the rising prices of everyday goods and the broader inflationary pressures felt in households across the country; for policymakers, it serves as a strategic wake-up call to reassess and reform trade policies to regain lost ground and protect national economic interests.

**De-Dollarization: A Long-Term Threat**

De-dollarization represents perhaps the most profound and existential challenge to America's financial architecture, as it

directly undermines the foundational privileges that come with the dollar's status as the world's reserve currency. This privileged position allows the United States to borrow capital at remarkably low interest rates—for instance, 10-year Treasury yields stood at 4.2% in 2025—and to enforce sanctions against adversaries with relative ease, leveraging the global dependence on dollar-based systems. However, the BRICS coalition's aggressive push to conduct trade in local currencies, supported by dedicated institutions such as the New Development Bank (NDB), is actively threatening this established order. The NDB, which has disbursed

$32 billion in loans by 2025, primarily funds infrastructure and development projects using yuan and rupees, thereby reducing the overall demand for dollars in international lending.

Complementing this is the Contingent Reserve Arrangement

(CRA), which provides access to $100 billion in emergency funds for member nations, positioning it as a credible rival to the International Monetary Fund (IMF) and offering an alternative safety net outside of Western influence.

Nevertheless, the process of de-dollarization is not without its significant limitations and hurdles. The Chinese yuan, for example, currently accounts for only 3.1% of global reserves, a figure that is constrained by China's stringent capital controls and the lingering lack of full global trust in its financial transparency and stability.

Estimates from the IMF indicate that intra-BRICS trade conducted in local currencies stands at just 20%, highlighting that the dollar's unparalleled liquidity and widespread acceptance continue to make it the preferred choice for many international transactions. In

Sarah's experience, her clients often revert to using dollars for larger or more complex deals, citing the currency's proven stability and ease of use as key factors. Despite these obstacles, the overarching trend is unmistakable: each additional deal settled in yuan or other local currencies incrementally chips away at the United States' financial leverage, creating cumulative effects over time. For students exploring the intersections of finance and geopolitics, this serves as an invaluable lesson in how monetary policies can shape power dynamics on the world stage; for policymakers, it frames the situation as a critical race against time to adapt and innovate before these shifts become irreversible.

**The Human Cost: Sarah's Struggle**

To truly grasp the implications of these economic shifts, it is essential to humanize the abstract data and statistics through stories like that of Sarah Martinez, whose personal experiences bring the broader trends into sharp, relatable focus. Her company, which was originally founded by her grandfather in the industrious 1950s and built upon the backbone of America's once-dominant manufacturing sector, has historically thrived due to the nation's economic might and global reach. Now, however, Sarah is forced to make difficult decisions, including laying off loyal workers as incoming orders continue to dwindle amid intensifying competition. Chinese competitors, bolstered by generous state subsidies and the efficient logistics provided through the Belt and Road Initiative, can offer steel products at prices that are 20% lower than what Sarah can match, putting her firm at a severe disadvantage. The adoption of the digital yuan further streamlines their business dealings, allowing for seamless and cost-effective

transactions, while Sarah's reliance on U.S. banks incurs high fees for currency conversions and adds layers of complexity to her operations.

Sarah's attempts to pivot her business toward alternative markets, such as those in Europe, have largely failed due to the dominance of BRICS-established trade routes and preferences that favor non-dollar systems. She often finds herself pondering whether her son

will inherit a viable, thriving business or merely an outdated relic of a bygone era of American industrial supremacy. This personal plight is reflective of much larger trends affecting the U.S. economy as a whole. According to data from the Bureau of Labor Statistics, the American manufacturing sector has shed approximately 2 million jobs since the turn of the millennium in 2000, a loss that has disproportionately impacted small and mid-

sized businesses like Sarah's, which collectively employ about 70% of the nation's workforce. These enterprises are grappling with escalating costs, contracting markets, and the need to adapt to a rapidly changing global landscape. For veterans such as Michael Sullivan, who was introduced in Chapter 1 and has witnessed the evolution of conflicts from physical battlefields to economic

arenas, Sarah's story draws clear parallels: it depicts a nation striving to hold its ground in a new form of warfare where resilience and adaptability are paramount. Yet, Sarah's own determination—evident in her exploration of new market opportunities and her active lobbying for protective tariffs—mirrors the potential for America as a whole to achieve renewal through perseverance and strategic foresight.

**Countering the Threat**

The realities of economic warfare necessitate a comprehensive and multifaceted response from the United States if it hopes to mitigate the ongoing threats and reclaim its position of strength. One key avenue for strengthening the dollar involves concerted efforts to reduce persistent budget deficits and make substantial investments in domestic industry to enhance productivity and competitiveness. Rebuilding resilient supply chains, as Sarah herself aspires to do for her business, would require targeted incentives such as tax breaks, grants, and regulatory reforms to encourage manufacturing on American soil and reduce reliance on imports. On the diplomatic front, the U.S. must actively counter the expansive

reach of China's Belt and Road Initiative by advancing its own alternative trade and investment frameworks, such as the Indo-Pacific Economic Framework, which aims to foster closer economic ties with allies in the region and promote standards that align with American values.

Furthermore, embracing financial innovation could prove instrumental in this fight; for instance, the development of a U.S.-backed digital dollar might effectively match the capabilities of China's e-CNY, providing a modern, efficient alternative that maintains the dollar's relevance in the digital age. While Chapter 9 will delve more extensively into these potential solutions and their implementation, the sense of urgency cannot be overstated—the time to act is now, before the window of opportunity narrows further. For veterans viewing this through the lens of strategic missions, this chapter positions economic warfare as a fresh assignment that demands disciplined strategy over emotional reactions or complacency. Students can glean important lessons on

how interconnected trade and currency policies fundamentally shape geopolitical power structures, while policymakers are equipped with actionable insights: the imperative to protect the dollar's status, to fundamentally rethink and reform trade strategies, and to invest heavily in building long-term economic resilience. Even for general readers like Sarah, who experience these dynamics through everyday impacts on their wallets and local communities, understanding these countermeasures offers hope and a pathway toward stability.

**Conclusion: A War Without End**

In summary, the domain of economic warfare—encompassing intense currency wars, profound shifts in trade patterns, and the gradual process of de-dollarization—poses a serious and

multifaceted threat to America's longstanding global dominance and financial preeminence. The rise of the BRICS coalition,

propelled by innovations like China's digital yuan and the development of alternative financial systems, is actively challenging the reign of the U.S. dollar and diminishing the leverage that the United States has historically wielded through its currency. The personal struggle of Sarah Martinez vividly illustrates the human toll exacted by these transformations, bringing to life the emotional and practical hardships faced by individuals and families, while the accompanying data and analyses underscore the immense strategic risks at play for the nation as a whole. Yet, much like the foundational cracks discussed in Chapter 1, this situation does not inevitably signal a terminal decline or an unavoidable defeat. Instead, the United States possesses the capacity to adapt and evolve—through well-crafted policies, technological innovations, and a unified national effort—to sustain its competitive edge and navigate these challenges successfully. The BRICS challenge, which was broadly outlined in Chapter 2, now manifests in tangible and concrete forms within these economic battles, but the prospects for

America's renewal ultimately depends on a willingness to confront these threats directly and decisively.

| **Year** | **U.S. Dollar** (%) | **Euro** (%) | **Chinese Yuan** (%) | **Other** (%) |
|---|---|---|---|---|
| 2000 | 71.1% | 18.3% | 0.0% | 10.6% |
| 2010 | 61.8% | 26.0% | 1.0% | 11.2% |
| 2020 | 59.2% | 20.5% | 2.3% | 18.0% |
| 2025 | 58.7% | 20.1% | 3.1% | 18.1% |

**Source:** IMF Currency Composition of Official Foreign Exchange Reserves, 2025 *(projected)*

# Chapter 4: The Military Gap

"You may fly over a land forever; you may bomb it, atomize it, pulverize it, and wipe it clean of life—but if you desire to defend it, protect it, and keep it for civilization, you must do this on the ground, the way the Roman legions did, by putting your young men in the mud."

***— Gen. Dwight D. Eisenhower, Address to Congress, 1951***

In the spring of 2025, Private First-Class Ethan Carter, a wide-eyed 19-year-old Army recruit from the heart of rural Georgia, stands rigidly at attention in the dusty training yard of Fort Benning, now known as Fort Moore. The relentless Georgia sun beats down, causing beads of sweat to trickle down his forehead and soak through his camouflage fatigues, making the heavy fabric cling uncomfortably to his skin. The drill sergeant's booming commands echo across the yard—"Left face! Forward march!"—but they barely penetrate Ethan's whirlwind of racing thoughts. Can I really hack this? he wonders silently, his mind drifting far from the repetitive drills. His unit is outfitted with standard-issue M4 rifles and a fleet of aging Humvees that rattle and groan with every maneuver, relics from a bygone era. Meanwhile, the news feeds he scrolls through on his phone during rare breaks are abuzz with reports of China's cutting-edge hypersonic missiles streaking across the skies at unimaginable speeds and Russia's sophisticated cyberwarfare drills that simulate crippling entire nations' infrastructures. Ethan, who spent his teenage years immersed in virtual gaming worlds, mastering complex strategies in online battles, finds himself grappling with equipment and tactics that feel archaic, trapped in a military culture seemingly stuck in the 20th century. He enlisted to serve his country, deeply inspired by his father's tales of valor from the Gulf War, where the elder Carter had fought with unwavering pride. But as the days grind on, doubts begin to creep in like shadows at dusk. The Army had missed its recruitment goals the previous year by a significant margin, and Ethan's platoon is operating at only half its authorized strength, leaving gaps in formations and overburdening the few who remain. He can't help but ponder: Is America's military, once hailed as the undisputed gold standard of global power, truly prepared for the escalating threats on the horizon?

This chapter delves deeply into the widening chasm in U.S. military capabilities, a gap exacerbated by a confluence of factors, including shrinking recruitment numbers, outdated readiness levels, and rapid technological advancements by adversarial nations such as China and Russia. Through the personal lens of

Ethan's story, we witness the profound human toll of these systemic challenges—the frustration, the uncertainty, and the quiet resilience of those on the front lines. Interwoven with this narrative are hard-hitting data points and analyses that illuminate the strategic risks facing the nation. We examine in detail the revolutionary impact of hypersonic weapons, the vulnerabilities in cyberwarfare defenses, and the pressing imperative for comprehensive modernization efforts. For veterans, this narrative resonates on a visceral level, echoing their own struggles during service and evoking a sense of shared hardship. For policymakers, it serves as a stark signal, a clarion call to action amid complacency. For students studying international relations or history, it offers a compelling lesson in the dynamics of national security, illustrating how internal weaknesses can undermine external strength. For active-duty military personnel, it holds up a mirror to their everyday realities, validating their experiences in an often-unforgiving system. Building upon the themes of economic warfare explored in Chapter 3, this chapter demonstrates how military vulnerabilities compound America's broader geopolitical decline, creating a feedback loop of diminishing influence. Yet, it also posits that through targeted strategic reforms, renewal is not only possible but achievable, offering a pathway out of the current predicament.

**The Recruitment Crisis: A Shrinking Force**

The foundation of the U.S. military's unparalleled strength has historically been its people—the dedicated men and women who volunteer to defend the nation. However, in recent years, recruitment has plunged into a profound crisis, threatening the very sustainability of this human backbone. In 2024, the Army fell short of its enlistment goal by a staggering 15,000 soldiers, bringing in only 55,000 recruits against a target of 70,000, as reported by the Department of Defense (DoD). This shortfall was not isolated; the Navy and Air Force encountered similar deficits, with recruitment numbers lagging by 10% and 12%, respectively. By 2025, the total active-duty force will have dwindled to approximately

1.3 million personnel, a notable decline from the 1.5 million who served in the year 2000. This contraction severely strains the military's capacity to sustain operations across its vast network of over 700 overseas bases and fulfill ongoing global commitments, from deterrence missions in the Indo-Pacific to stabilization efforts in the Middle East.

Ethan Carter's personal journey encapsulates the multifaceted causes behind this recruitment downturn. In a robust economy where unemployment hovers at a low 3.8% in 2025, according to the Bureau of Labor Statistics, young Americans like Ethan are presented with an array of better-paying civilian opportunities that promise financial stability without the rigors of military life.

Generation Z, to which Ethan belongs, exhibits a marked decline in trust toward traditional institutions; a 2024 Gallup poll reveals that only 43% of this demographic views the military favorably, a sharp drop from the 60% approval rating it enjoyed in 2000. This erosion of confidence is amplified by the pervasive influence of social media platforms, where X (formerly Twitter) posts frequently criticize military scandals, such as sexual assault cases or the mishandling of veteran benefits, alongside endless debates about protracted wars in Afghanistan and Iraq. Ethan himself was drawn to enlistment by the allure of college benefits through the GI Bill and a deeper sense of purpose. Still, he quickly discovers that basic training is a grueling ordeal, disconnected from the technological demands of contemporary warfare. His peers, who grew up with artificial intelligence assistants and virtual reality simulations as everyday tools, perceive the military as an anachronistic institution, ill-equipped to harness their digital-native skills.

Demographic trends further compound the recruitment woes, painting a picture of a narrowing pipeline of potential enlistees. The U.S. youth population in the prime recruitment age bracket of 18–24 is shrinking due to persistently low birth rates over the past decades, resulting in fewer eligible candidates overall. A comprehensive 2024 DoD study highlights that only about 9% of this age group meets the stringent criteria for service, factoring in issues related to physical fitness, educational attainment, and criminal records. Alarmingly, obesity rates among young adults have climbed to 42%, disqualifying a substantial portion from even

basic eligibility. For veterans like Ethan's father, who served with a profound sense of duty and sacrifice, this crisis feels like a profound betrayal—a dilution of the ethos that once defined American patriotism. For policymakers, it represents a critical strategic liability, necessitating immediate interventions such as enhanced compensation packages, streamlined enlistment processes, or innovative training programs that integrate modern technology to appeal to younger generations. Without these fixes, the military risks becoming a hollow force, unable to project power effectively in an increasingly multipolar world.

**Outdated Readiness: A Force Stretched Thin**

Military readiness, defined as the capacity to deploy forces swiftly and sustain effective combat operations, is undergoing a troubling erosion that undermines America's defense posture. Despite boasting the world's largest defense budget at $850 billion in 2025, the allocation of funds reveals inherent inefficiencies: approximately 60% is devoted to personnel costs and routine maintenance, leaving a mere $340 billion for critical modernization initiatives, as outlined by the Congressional Budget Office. This budgetary skew perpetuates the persistence of aging equipment across all branches, hampering operational effectiveness. For instance, 40% of the Army's vehicles, including the Humvees that Ethan trains with, are over two decades old, prone to breakdowns, and requiring constant repairs. Similarly,

70% of the Air Force's aircraft fleet, such as the venerable F-16 fighters, date back to before 1990, facing obsolescence in the face of newer threats. The Navy, with its current inventory of 290 ships—a drastic reduction from the 600 vessels it maintained in 1980—struggles to maintain presence in key maritime domains like the South China Sea.

Ethan's firsthand experiences during training vividly expose these readiness gaps, turning abstract statistics into tangible frustrations. His platoon relies on outdated simulators from the early 2000s, which pale in comparison to the advanced AI-driven training systems employed by Chinese forces, where virtual scenarios adapt in real-time to soldier inputs. Maintenance backlogs are a constant issue; in Ethan's unit, half the helicopters are grounded due to parts shortages or mechanical failures, a microcosm of broader problems identified in a 2024 RAND Corporation report that deemed 30% of all U.S. aircraft non-mission-capable at any given time. Compounding these internal challenges are the demands of extensive overseas commitments: American troops remain deployed in hotspots like Syria for counterterrorism operations, South Korea for deterrence against North Korean aggression, and various European nations to bolster NATO alliances amid Russian threats. The protracted conflicts in Iraq and Afghanistan, which have cumulatively cost over $6 trillion and claimed more than 7,000 American lives, have not only depleted financial resources but also eroded public support, fostering a war-

weary populace. On social media platforms like X, 2025 posts from disillusioned citizens and service members' alike vent

frustrations: "Why are we still entangled in the Middle East when our own gear is falling apart at home?" These sentiments reflect a growing disconnect between military obligations and domestic priorities.

For active-duty troops like Ethan, this outdated readiness translates to a daily grind of improvisation and overwork, where ingenuity must compensate for inadequate resources. Policymakers are confronted with the imperative to reallocate budgets more strategically, perhaps by prioritizing procurement of next-generation platforms over sustaining legacy systems. Students analyzing national security can observe a military apparatus struggling to adapt to the pace of global change, highlighting the dangers of complacency in an era of rapid evolution. Veterans, reflecting on their own eras of service, often recall a time when readiness was assumed rather than questioned, underscoring the need for a return to that foundational strength through deliberate investment and reform.

**Technological Lag: Losing the Edge**

Once the unchallenged leader in military innovation, America's technological superiority is now on the brink, with rivals like China and Russia making concerted investments to close and, in some cases, surpass the gap. The following table provides a comparative overview of U.S. and Chinese military capabilities as of 2025, drawing from authoritative sources to illustrate the shifting balance:

| **Category** | **United States** | **China** |
|---|---|---|
| Defense Budget | $850 billion | $300 billion |
| Active Personnel | 1.3 million | 2.0 million |
| Naval Ships | 290 | 340 |
| Fighter Aircraft | 2,600 (30% 5th-gen, e.g., F-35) | 1,900 (20% 5th-gen, e.g., J-20) |
| Hypersonic Missiles | 10 test models | 50+ deployed |
| Cyber Units | 133 (Cyber Command) | 200+ (PLA Strategic Support) |
| AI/Drone Systems | 1,200 drones, early AI adoption | 2,000+ drones, advanced AI |

Source: DoD, Center for Strategic and International Studies (CSIS), and International Institute for Strategic Studies (IISS) Military Balance, 2025.

This data underscores a narrative of convergence, where China's lower budget yields disproportionate gains through focused priorities on asymmetric capabilities.

**Hypersonic Weapons**

Hypersonic weapons represent a paradigm shift in missile technology, capable of traveling at speeds exceeding Mach 5—over 3,800 miles per hour—while maneuvering unpredictably to evade traditional defense systems. China's DF-ZF hypersonic glide vehicle, operational since 2020, exemplifies this threat, enabling strikes on targets up to 2,000 miles away in mere minutes, potentially neutralizing carrier strike groups or island bases. Russia has demonstrated its Kinzhal air-launched hypersonic missile in real-world scenarios during the Ukraine conflict, proving its ability to penetrate advanced air defenses. In contrast, the United States lags significantly; its programs, such as the Army's Long-Range Hypersonic Weapon, remain in developmental stages, with full deployment delayed until at least 2026, as detailed in a 2024 Government Accountability Office (GAO) report citing technical hurdles and supply chain issues. During Ethan's training sessions, instructors mention hypersonics only in brief, theoretical terms, without providing hands-on countermeasures or simulations, leaving recruits like him feeling vulnerable and unprepared for a future battlefield where such weapons could dominate. This disparity not only heightens the risk of deterrence failure but also forces U.S. planners to rethink doctrines reliant on legacy interceptors like the Patriot system, which are ill-suited to hypersonic velocities.

**Cyberwarfare Gaps**

The domain of cyberwarfare has emerged as a critical battleground, where invisible attacks can inflict damage comparable to kinetic strikes. China's People's Liberation Army (PLA) Strategic Support Force, boasting over 200,000 dedicated personnel, has honed sophisticated cyber capabilities, evidenced by incidents like the 2023 breach of U.S. Navy systems that compromised sensitive ship designs, according to a 2024 CSIS analysis. Russia's GRU intelligence unit has conducted disruptive operations, including simulated takedowns of U.S. power grids in 2024 exercises that highlighted vulnerabilities in critical infrastructure. The U.S. Cyber Command, with its 133 operational teams, faces significant hurdles, including outdated protocols and an acute shortage of around 20,000 cyber specialists, as noted in a 2025 DoD workforce report. Recruitment in this field is hampered by competition from the private sector, where salaries for cybersecurity experts often exceed $150,000 annually. Ethan, who dabbled in coding and ethical hacking during high school to mod video games, encounters Army cyber training that feels rudimentary and disconnected from the AI-enhanced threats proliferating online. Discussions on X about recent hacks amplify his concerns, with users sharing analyses of how adversaries use machine learning to automate intrusions. This gap exposes U.S. networks to exploitation, potentially disrupting command and control during conflicts and eroding the information superiority that has long been an American hallmark.

Beyond hypersonics and cyber, China's advancements in artificial intelligence and unmanned systems further tilt the scales. The dominance of Chinese firms like DJI in the global drone market—controlling 80% of commercial sales—translates to military advantages, with variants capable of swarming in coordinated attacks. The U.S. fields about 1,200 drones, but only 10% possess true autonomy, lagging behind China's 2,000+ units, where half incorporate advanced AI for decision-making. For students, these developments serve as a vivid illustration of how technology is reshaping the nature of warfare, from symmetric confrontations to hybrid threats. Policymakers must heed this as an urgent prompt for increased research and development funding, fostering collaborations with academia and industry to regain the initiative.

**Ethan's Struggle: A Recruit's Perspective**

At the heart of these macro-level challenges lies the intimate story of Ethan Carter, a narrative that humanizes the cold statistics and brings the crisis into sharp, personal focus. Growing up in a modest home in rural Georgia, surrounded by rolling fields and small-town simplicity, Ethan was shaped by his father's Gulf War stories—tales of camaraderie under fire, the thrill of victory, and the weight of sacrifice. Seeking to escape a dead-end job at a local warehouse and to honor that legacy, Ethan enlisted, envisioning a path to purpose and education. However, basic training at Fort Moore unfolds like a journey through a time warp: drills emphasize marksmanship with M16 rifles rather than piloting drones or navigating augmented reality battlefields. His platoon, chronically understaffed and perpetually overworked, contends with equipment that his father would recognize from the 1990s—rusty bayonets, analog radios, and vehicles that break down during exercises. The physical demands are relentless: endless push-ups in the mud, long ruck marches under heavy loads, and sleep-deprived nights that test resolve. Ethan's tech-savvy comrades, accustomed to seamless digital interfaces, begin to drop out one by one, disillusioned by the bureaucracy, rigid hierarchies, and meager starting salaries of around $25,000 per year. In comparison, entry-level tech jobs in Silicon Valley or Atlanta offer upwards of $80,000, with perks like flexible hours and no mandatory physical exertion. A viral 2024 X post that Ethan stumbled upon during a brief phone break encapsulates the

sentiment: "Why join the Army when Silicon Valley pays better and doesn't make you run in the rain? #MilitaryLife

#GenZStruggles"

Ethan's internal conflicts intensify during a particularly eye-opening cyber training module. The instructor, a grizzled veteran of multiple tours in Iraq, delivers the material with earnestness but admits outright that U.S. systems lag far behind those of China and Russia in sophistication and resilience. Ethan, recalling his teenage exploits in hacking game servers for fun (always ethically, he assures himself), can't help but question why the Army isn't better leveraging talents like his. Why aren't there more programs to integrate coders, gamers, and innovators directly into cyber units? These doubts swirl as he lies in his bunk at night, staring at the ceiling, weighing his sense of duty against the growing realization that the institution he serves may not be evolving fast enough. Yet, amidst the uncertainty, Ethan persists, fueled by an innate resilience and a flickering hope that reforms are on the way. His platoon mates share similar stories—some from urban backgrounds, others from military families—all grappling with the same disconnect between their expectations and reality. Ethan's experience mirrors the broader state of America's military: beleaguered and strained, yet endowed with a core of dedicated individuals who refuse to yield. It underscores the need for leadership to bridge the generational divide, perhaps by incorporating virtual training platforms or gamified recruitment strategies that resonate with digital natives.

### The Path to Modernization

Confronting and closing the military capability gap demands bold, multifaceted action from all stakeholders, transforming challenges into opportunities for resurgence. To stem the recruitment hemorrhage, initiatives must focus on making service more appealing to contemporary youth. This could involve competitive pay raises, perhaps benchmarking salaries against private-sector equivalents, alongside tech-infused training curricula that incorporate virtual reality simulations and AI-assisted drills.

Outreach efforts should leverage platforms like X, TikTok, and Instagram, where Gen Z congregates, to showcase modern military roles—cyber warriors, drone operators, and data analysts—rather than traditional infantry stereotypes. Additionally, addressing eligibility barriers through partnerships with schools for fitness programs or educational outreach could expand the pool of qualified candidates.

Enhancing readiness requires a fundamental reallocation of resources within the bloated defense budget. Policymakers could consider scaling back the footprint of overseas bases, which number over 700 and consume vast sums in logistics and maintenance, redirecting those funds toward procuring state-of-the-art equipment. For example, accelerating the replacement of aging Humvees with next-generation joint light tactical vehicles or upgrading aircraft fleets to include more unmanned systems would alleviate current strains. Investments in predictive maintenance technologies, powered by AI, could reduce downtime and extend the lifespan of existing assets, as suggested by various think tank reports.

To counter the technological lag, a massive infusion of research and development funding is essential—potentially $50 billion annually, as recommended in a 2024 Brookings Institution study—to accelerate progress in hypersonics, cyber defenses, and AI. This could involve forging deeper partnerships with innovative private-sector firms like Palantir for data analytics, SpaceX for advanced rocketry, or Google for AI applications, bridging the gap between Silicon Valley's agility and the Pentagon's scale. Incentives such as tax breaks or streamlined contracting could encourage tech talent to contribute to national defense, addressing shortages in cyber and engineering fields.

For veterans, this chapter stirs a complex mix of emotions: pride in their past service juxtaposed with frustration over the evident decline, motivating advocacy for change. Active-duty personnel like Ethan find their daily challenges validated, fostering a sense of solidarity and urgency. Students gain insights into how technological disruptions are redefining warfare, from the Industrial Revolution's impact on tactics to today's digital transformations. Policymakers are presented with a clear mandate: act decisively to modernize, or risk ceding ground irretrievably.

While Chapter 9 will outline specific reform blueprints in greater detail, the message here is unequivocal—the window for action is narrowing, and the stakes could not be higher.

**Conclusion: A Call to Arms**

The fissures in the U.S. military—manifested through dwindling recruitment, eroding readiness, and a diminishing technological edge—pose an existential threat to its longstanding global dominance. As China and Russia surge ahead with breakthroughs in hypersonic missiles and cyberwarfare capabilities, America's overstretched and under-resourced forces amplify the vulnerabilities highlighted in the economic warfare discussions of Chapters 1 through 3. Ethan Carter's personal odyssey illuminates the human dimension of this crisis, where individual aspirations collide with institutional shortcomings, while empirical data lay bare the strategic perils of inaction. Nevertheless, as President

Dwight D. Eisenhower once articulated, a nation's true strength resides not merely in its armaments but in the resolve and ingenuity of its people. Through concerted modernization efforts, innovative policies, and a renewed national commitment, these gaps can be bridged, affirming the central thesis of this book: America's geopolitical decline, though palpable and multifaceted, is not inevitable but rather a reversible trajectory contingent upon bold, decisive action.

# Chapter 5: Terror in the Shadows

"The threats we face today are not just from armies or ideologies, but from the shadows—where technology and malice converge to strike at the heart of our way of life."
***— Robert Kagan, The World America Made***

On a crisp October morning in 2025, the city of Charlotte, North Carolina, awakens to chaos. Traffic lights flicker erratically, their signals cycling between green and red without logic, stranding commuters in gridlock. Hospital systems crash, leaving doctors unable to access patient records, forcing them to resort to pen and paper in a frantic bid to maintain care. Bank ATMs across the city flash error messages, denying residents access to cash and digital transactions. At Charlotte-Douglas International Airport, Sarah Martinez, the Pittsburgh-based business owner introduced in Chapter 3, finds herself stranded, her flight grounded as air traffic control systems succumb to a mysterious failure. Her phone buzzes incessantly with alerts: a ransomware attack, traced to a shadowy group linked to Iranian proxies, has crippled the city's critical infrastructure. Power outages spread like wildfire, plunging neighborhoods into darkness, while panic ripples through posts on

X, where residents share frantic updates and demand answers from local authorities. For Sarah, it's a personal crisis that threatens her business and livelihood; for the nation, it's a stark wake-up call.

This isn't the terrorism of 9/11, with its devastating physical toll—it's a silent, digital assault, exploiting America's interconnected vulnerabilities in a new era of warfare.

This chapter delves into the evolving landscape of global terrorism, focusing on the rise of cyberthreats, asymmetric warfare, and the growing influence of non-state actors and state-sponsored attacks. Through the lens of the Charlotte cyberattack, we explore how these threats challenge U.S. national security in ways that traditional military strategies are ill-equipped to counter. The shift from the physical destruction of al-Qaeda's 2001 attacks to the decentralized, tech-driven assaults of 2025 reveals a new paradigm of terrorism—one that leverages technology to maximize disruption with minimal resources. For military readers, this chapter highlights the operational challenges of defending against invisible enemies on digital battlefields. For students, it serves as a case study in the dynamics of modern threat landscapes. For

policymakers, it's a clarion call to fortify America's defenses against a rapidly evolving adversary. Building on the military gaps identified in Chapter 4, this chapter illustrates how terror in the

shadows deepens America's geopolitical decline, while offering a roadmap for renewal through proactive measures in cybersecurity, infrastructure resilience, and strategic adaptation.

### The Evolution of Terrorism: From Physical to Digital Destruction

The landscape of global terrorism has undergone a profound transformation since the catastrophic attacks of September 11, 2001, when al-Qaeda's coordinated assault on the World Trade Center and Pentagon killed 2,977 people and reshaped U.S. national security policy. Those attacks relied on physical destruction—hijacked planes, explosives, and meticulous planning—to achieve maximum psychological and economic impact. In the decades since, terrorist organizations have adapted to a rapidly changing technological landscape, moving away from spectacular, large-scale physical attacks toward decentralized, tech-driven operations that exploit the vulnerabilities of a hyper-connected world. By 2025, non-state actors such as ISIS-K, Boko Haram, and hacktivist collectives like Anonymous, alongside state-backed groups from adversarial nations like Russia, China,

Iran and North Korea have embraced digital tools to wage asymmetric warfare—attacks that deliver disproportionate damage relative to the resources invested.

According to a 2025 report from the Center for Strategic and International Studies (CSIS), global terrorist incidents have declined from a peak of 12,000 in 2015 to approximately 8,000 in 2024. However, this reduction in frequency belies a troubling increase in the lethality and economic impact of these attacks,

driven by the integration of advanced technology. Cyberattacks, in particular, have emerged as a preferred method for both non-state and state-sponsored actors, capable of paralyzing entire cities or industries without firing a single shot. The Charlotte ransomware attacks, orchestrated by a group known as Dark Crescent, exemplify this evolution. Unlike the 9/11 attacks, which required years of planning and physical operatives, the Charlotte attack is executed remotely by a small team of hackers, likely fewer than a dozen, using off-the-shelf malware to lock critical systems across the city. The ransom demand—$50 million in untraceable cryptocurrency—underscores the financial motivations that often accompany these digital assaults, blending ideological goals with profiteering.

The impact of the Charlotte attack is staggering. While it causes no immediate casualties, it paralyzes a city of 900,000 residents, disrupting essential services and costing an estimated $1 billion per day in economic losses, according to a 2025 FEMA analysis.

Businesses grind to a halt, supply chains stall, and public confidence erodes as residents grapple with the sudden loss of basic services. Sarah Martinez, stranded at the airport, watches helplessly as her Pittsburgh-based business, reliant on cloud-based systems for inventory and payroll, becomes inaccessible. Her suppliers, unable to process orders, delay shipments, threatening

her company's viability. On X, Charlotte residents amplify the chaos, with one viral thread declaring, "This is war without bombs—a silent invasion." For military readers, this scenario underscores the emergence of a new battlefield, where traditional tactics are obsolete, and cyber defenses are as critical as physical ones. For students, the Charlotte attack serves as a vivid case study in the evolution of terrorism, illustrating how technology has democratized destruction, enabling small groups to wield outsized influence. For policymakers, it highlights the urgent need to

address America's digital vulnerabilities before they are exploited further.

The shift to digital terrorism is not merely a change in tactics but a fundamental redefinition of warfare itself. Traditional terrorism relied on physical presence—suicide bombers, hijackers, or armed militants—to achieve its aims. In contrast, cyberterrorism operates in the shadows, exploiting the interconnectedness of modern infrastructure to create cascading failures. A single breach can disrupt multiple sectors simultaneously, as seen in Charlotte, where power outages, grounded flights, and offline hospitals create a domino effect of chaos. This evolution reflects a broader trend: adversaries no longer need to match America's military might to inflict harm. Instead, they target its soft underbelly—its reliance on digital systems and aging infrastructure—to achieve strategic objectives. The Charlotte attack, while localized, sends ripples across the nation, exposing the fragility of systems that Americans take for granted.

### Non-State Actors: The Shadow Warriors of the Digital Age

Non-state actors have become the vanguard of this new era of terrorism, leveraging technology to amplify their reach and impact. Groups like ISIS-K, operating from strongholds in Afghanistan, have adapted to the digital age, using encrypted platforms like Telegram to recruit operatives, coordinate attacks, and spread propaganda. By 2025, the United Nations Security Council estimates that ISIS-K has grown to 10,000 operatives globally, a testament to its ability to operate across borders without a centralized command structure. The group's 2024 bombing of a Moscow concert hall, which killed 133 people and injured hundreds more, demonstrated its capacity to strike distant targets with precision and brutality. Similarly, groups like Boko Haram in Nigeria and al-Shabaab in Somalia have integrated technology into their operations, using drones and social media to expand their influence beyond their immediate regions.

Hacktivist collectives, such as Anonymous, represent another facet of non-state threats. These loosely organized groups use cyberattacks to target governments, corporations, and institutions, often in pursuit of ideological goals. In 2023, Anonymous claimed responsibility for a breach of sensitive U.S. defense contractor files, leaking classified documents on X to expose perceived government overreach. While their actions lack the physical violence of groups like ISIS-K, their ability to disrupt and embarrass powerful institutions makes them a significant threat. The decentralized nature of hacktivist groups—operating without a clear hierarchy or fixed location—makes them difficult to counter, as traditional law enforcement and military strategies are ill-suited to tracking amorphous, online entities.

The Charlotte attack highlights how non-state actors' exploit

America's digital vulnerabilities. The Department of Homeland Security (DHS) reports that 80% of U.S. critical infrastructure—encompassing power grids, water treatment facilities, hospitals, and transportation systems—is privately owned and often inadequately protected. This patchwork of ownership creates gaps that groups like Dark Crescent can exploit with relative ease. In Charlotte, the ransomware attack targets hospitals, utilities, and financial systems, all of which rely on interconnected networks with minimal redundancy. Sarah Martinez's experience underscores the human toll: when she seeks medical care for a stranded employee at a Charlotte hospital, she finds the facility in disarray, its electronic health records inaccessible and backup systems nonexistent. For veterans reading this chapter, the tactics of non-state actors evoke memories of guerrilla warfare, where small, agile forces exploit the weaknesses of larger, conventional armies. For policymakers, the reliance on private infrastructure demands urgent action to foster public-private partnerships, ensuring that critical systems are fortified against digital threats.

The adaptability of non-state actors is a key factor in their success. Unlike state militaries, which are bound by bureaucracy and resource constraints, these groups operate with agility, leveraging commercially available technology to devastating effect. For example, consumer drones, costing as little as $1,000, have been weaponized by groups like the Houthis in Yemen to disrupt global shipping lanes. In 2024, Houthi drone attacks on Red Sea vessels cost the global economy $100 billion, according to the World Bank, by forcing ships to reroute around conflict zones. Similarly, ransomware tools, available on the dark web for a few hundred dollars, enable groups like Dark Crescent to hold entire cities hostage. This democratization of technology has lowered the barriers to entry for terrorism, allowing small groups to achieve strategic impacts once reserved for state actors.

**State-Sponsored Cyberattacks: The Hidden Hand Behind the Chaos**

While non-state actors pose a significant threat, state-sponsored cyberattacks represent a far graver challenge to U.S. national security. Adversarial nations like Russia, China, Iran, and North Korea have developed sophisticated cyber units designed to target critical infrastructure, steal sensitive data, and sow discord. The Charlotte attack, linked to Iran's Islamic Revolutionary Guard Corps (IRGC) through its proxy group Dark Crescent, follows a well-established pattern of state-backed cyber operations. In 2023,

China's Volt Typhoon cyber unit infiltrated U.S. power grids, remaining undetected for months and laying the groundwork for potential widespread outages, according to a Microsoft report.

Russia's GRU, responsible for the 2020 SolarWinds attack that compromised 18,000 organizations worldwide, disrupted 20% of Ukraine's digital infrastructure in 2024, providing a blueprint for similar attacks on U.S. targets. North Korea's Lazarus Group, meanwhile, has focused on financial gain, stealing $600 million in

Cryptocurrency in 2024 to fund its nuclear weapons program, according to a Chainalysis report.

Their sophistication and strategic intent characterize these state-sponsored attacks. Unlike the opportunistic strikes of non-state actors, state-backed operations are often part of broader geopolitical strategies aimed at weakening adversaries, testing defenses, or extracting resources. For example, Russia's 2024 disruption of Ukraine's infrastructure was designed to undermine public morale and cripple military logistics, a tactic that could be replicated against U.S. cities like Charlotte. Iran, facing economic sanctions and diplomatic isolation, uses proxies like Dark Crescent to strike at Western targets without direct attribution, complicating retaliation. The Charlotte attack, traced to servers in Eastern Europe, exemplifies this strategy: the use of intermediaries obscures the trail, delaying response and sowing confusion.

The following infographic (described in text for Markdown) summarizes major cyberattacks from 2015 to 2025, illustrating the growing scope and impact of state-sponsored operations:

**Major Cyberattacks (2015–2025)**

- **2015: OPM Breach (China)** – Stole 21.5 million U.S. government personnel records, compromising sensitive national security data.

- **2017: WannaCry Ransomware (North Korea)** – Affected 200,000 systems globally, causing $4 billion in damages to healthcare and businesses.

- **2020: SolarWinds Attack (Russia)** – Compromised 18,000 organizations, including U.S. government agencies, exposing critical networks.

- **2023: Volt Typhoon (China)** – Infiltrated U.S. power grids, undetected for months, with potential for widespread outages.

- **2024: Colonial Pipeline Hack (Russia-linked)** – Disrupted 45% of U.S. East Coast fuel supply, causing $1 billion in economic losses.

- **2025: Charlotte Ransomware (Iran-linked)** – Paralyzed city infrastructure, resulting in $1 billion daily economic

losses.
**Source**: CSIS, DHS, and FBI Cyber Division, 2025.

These attacks exploit systemic weaknesses in U.S. cybersecurity. The National Institute of Standards and Technology (NIST) reports that 60% of U.S. companies lack basic cyber defenses, such as multi-factor authentication or regular software updates. The Department of Defense (DoD), as noted in Chapter 4, operates 133 cyber teams but faces a shortfall of 20,000 specialists, hamstrung by competition with private tech firms offering higher salaries.

Small businesses like Sarah's are particularly vulnerable, often relying on outdated cloud systems with minimal security. For students, this data underscores the scope and complexity of cyberwarfare; for military leaders, it highlights the urgent need for operational enhancements, including recruitment and training of cyber specialists to counter state-backed threats.

State-sponsored cyberattacks also exploit the global nature of the internet, where borders are meaningless, and attribution is

challenging. The FBI's efforts to trace the Charlotte attack to Iran are hampered by the use of proxy servers and encrypted communications, delaying response and allowing the perpetrators to evade immediate consequences. This cat-and-mouse game underscores the need for international cooperation to combat cyberterrorism, as adversaries exploit jurisdictions with weak cybersecurity laws to launch attacks. For policymakers, this necessitates diplomatic efforts to establish global norms and consequences for state-sponsored cyber operations, a challenge complicated by geopolitical rivalries.

**U.S. Vulnerabilities: A Digital Achilles' Heel**

America's digital infrastructure is a patchwork of vulnerabilities, ripe for exploitation by both state and non-state actors. The Cybersecurity and Infrastructure Security Agency (CISA) identifies 16 critical infrastructure sectors—energy, finance, healthcare, transportation, and more—where a single breach can trigger cascading failures. The Charlotte attack demonstrates this fragility: the ransomware disrupts power grids, grounds flights, and paralyzes hospitals, creating a domino effect that amplifies the initial impact. A 2024 CISA report notes that 70% of U.S. power grids rely on outdated software, vulnerable to ransomware and other exploits. Similarly, 90% of U.S. financial transactions depend on digital systems with single points of failure, as Sarah

discovers when she's unable to access her bank accounts to pay suppliers or employees.

Physical infrastructure is equally at risk. The American Society of Civil Engineers (ASCE) gave U.S. infrastructure a C- grade in 2025, estimating that $2 trillion is needed to modernize aging systems. In Charlotte, backup generators fail due to underinvestment, leaving hospitals and emergency services crippled. This echoes the 2023 Texas grid collapse, where extreme weather exposed the fragility of unmaintained systems. X posts during the Charlotte attack capture public frustration, with one user lamenting, "Why can't we protect our own cities? This is a failure of leadership." For policymakers, this underscores the need for significant investment in infrastructure resilience, including

redundant systems and modernized grids. For general readers, it's a stark reminder of how disruptions to critical systems can upend daily life, from accessing money to receiving medical care.

The interconnectedness of America's infrastructure exacerbates these vulnerabilities. A single breach in one sector—such as energy—can ripple across others, as seen in Charlotte when power outages disrupt transportation and healthcare. The reliance on private companies to manage critical infrastructure further complicates the issue, as profit-driven firms often prioritize cost-cutting over security. Sarah's business, for example, uses a third-party cloud provider that lacks robust encryption, making it an easy target for ransomware. The broader implications are clear: without coordinated efforts to secure both digital and physical infrastructure, the U.S. remains exposed to attacks that can paralyze entire regions.

**Asymmetric Warfare: The New Normal in Global Conflict**

Asymmetric warfare—using unconventional means to counter superior forces—has become the hallmark of modern terrorism. Non-state actors leverage low-cost technologies to achieve outsized impacts, much like insurgents using improvised explosive devices (IEDs) against advanced militaries in Iraq and Afghanistan. In 2024, Houthi rebels in Yemen used $1,000 drones to disrupt Red Sea shipping, costing global trade $100 billion by forcing ships to reroute, according to the World Bank. Similarly,

state actors amplify these tactics: Iran's proxies, such as Hezbollah, deploy precision-guided munitions to target Israeli infrastructure, while Russia's Wagner Group uses disinformation campaigns to destabilize African governments, sowing chaos without deploying large forces.

The Charlotte attack is a textbook example of asymmetric warfare. A small team of hackers, likely fewer than 10, uses widely available ransomware to cripple a city of 900,000, causing $5 billion in economic damages over a week, per a 2025 Deloitte study. The attack's success lies in its simplicity: by targeting interconnected systems, the hackers create widespread disruption with minimal resources. The FBI's investigation traces Dark Crescent to servers in Eastern Europe, but the group's use of encrypted networks and proxy servers complicates attribution, delaying response and allowing the perpetrators to evade immediate consequences. For military readers, this mirrors the challenges of counterinsurgency, where identifying and neutralizing elusive enemies requires new strategies. For students, it's a lesson in how low-cost, high-impact tactics have reshaped modern warfare.

Asymmetric warfare also thrives on psychological impact. The Charlotte attack, while causing no direct casualties, erodes public trust in institutions, as residents question why their government failed to protect critical systems. X posts amplify this sentiment, with hashtags like #CharlotteChaos trending as users share images of darkened streets and stranded travelers. The psychological toll is compounded by economic disruption: businesses like Sarah's face supply chain delays, lost revenue, and employee hardship, creating a sense of vulnerability that adversaries exploit to weaken societal cohesion.

## Sarah's Ordeal: The Human Cost of Cyberterrorism

Sarah Martinez's experience in Charlotte personalizes the broader implications of the cyberattack. Stranded at Charlotte-Douglas International Airport, she watches helplessly as her Pittsburgh-based business grinds to a halt. Her company's cloud-based systems, used for inventory management and payroll, are locked by the ransomware, preventing her from processing orders or paying employees. Suppliers, caught in the same digital quagmire, delay shipments, threatening her business's survival. At a local hospital, where Sarah seeks care for a sick employee, the situation is dire: electronic health records are inaccessible, and backup systems are either nonexistent or overwhelmed, delaying treatment and heightening panic.

Sarah's frustration spills over onto X, where she posts from her hotel room: "This isn't just a hack—it's an attack on our way of

life. How are we supposed to function when everything we rely on is digital?" Her words resonate with thousands of Charlotte residents, whose posts amplify the sense of betrayal and vulnerability. The attack disrupts 50,000 businesses in the city, costing $5 billion in a single week, according to a 2025 Deloitte study. For veterans like Michael Sullivan, introduced in Chapter 1, the disruption recalls the chaos of wartime supply chain failures, where logistics breakdowns could paralyze entire operations. For Sarah, a resilient entrepreneur, the crisis is a test of endurance: she begins exploring cybersecurity upgrades for her business, determined to rebuild stronger.

Sarah's ordeal underscores the human cost of cyberterrorism. While the attack causes no physical casualties, its economic and emotional toll is profound. Employees unable to access payroll face financial hardship, with some, like Sarah's workers, receiving eviction notices as bills pile up. The hospital's failure to provide timely care exacerbates health risks, particularly for vulnerable populations. For general readers, Sarah's story makes the abstract threat of cyberterrorism tangible, illustrating how a single attack can ripple through communities, disrupting lives and livelihoods. Her determination to adapt—researching cybersecurity solutions and advocating for resilience—mirrors the broader potential for America to recover and strengthen its defenses.

**Countering the Threat: A Multi-Pronged Approach**

Addressing the rise of cyberterrorism and asymmetric warfare requires a comprehensive, multi-pronged strategy that spans cybersecurity, infrastructure investment, and international diplomacy. First, cybersecurity must be prioritized at both the national and local levels. The Cybersecurity and Infrastructure Security Agency (CISA) requires an estimated $10 billion annually to secure critical infrastructure, according to a 2024 Brookings Institution report. This funding would support the development of standardized cybersecurity protocols, mandatory for private companies managing critical systems. Public-private partnerships are essential to bridge the gap between government oversight and private-sector innovation, ensuring that firms like Sarah's have access to affordable, robust defenses.

The Department of Defense must also address its cyber workforce shortage. As noted in Chapter 4, the DoD's 133 cyber teams are understaffed by 20,000 specialists, a gap exacerbated by competition with tech giants offering salaries up to $500,000 annually. To close this gap, the DoD should implement aggressive recruitment campaigns, offering competitive pay, educational incentives, and clear career paths for cyber specialists. Investments in training programs, including partnerships with universities and tech companies, can build a pipeline of skilled professionals capable of defending against sophisticated state-sponsored attacks.

Infrastructure resilience is another critical priority. The ASCE's 2025 report estimates that $500 billion is needed to modernize power grids, hospitals, and transportation systems, reducing vulnerabilities like those exposed in Charlotte. Redundant systems, such as backup generators and offline data storage, can mitigate the impact of cyberattacks, ensuring that essential services remain operational. For policymakers, this requires reallocating federal budgets to prioritize infrastructure, potentially through public-private financing models that incentivize private investment in critical systems.

Diplomatically, the U.S. must deter state-sponsored cyberattacks through a combination of sanctions, international coalitions, and offensive cyber operations. The 2022 sanctions on Iran and Russia, targeting their financial systems, demonstrated the power of economic leverage, but their effectiveness depends on maintaining dollar dominance, as discussed in Chapter 3's exploration of economic warfare. International agreements on cyber norms, while challenging to enforce, could establish consequences for state-backed attacks, reducing the impunity enjoyed by groups like Dark

Crescent. For military readers, this necessitates modernizing defense strategies to prioritize cyber and drone defenses, integrating them into existing frameworks to counter hybrid threats.

Finally, public awareness and education are critical to building societal resilience. Initiatives to train small businesses and individuals in basic cybersecurity practices—such as multi-factor authentication and regular software updates—can reduce the attack surface for adversaries. Sarah's decision to invest in cybersecurity upgrades reflects the potential for grassroots resilience, but scaling this effort requires government support, including subsidies for small businesses to adopt secure systems.

**Conclusion: Facing the Shadows**

The evolution of global terrorism into a digital and asymmetric threat has reshaped the landscape of U.S. national security. The Charlotte ransomware attack, driven by non-state actors and state-sponsored proxies, reveals the stakes: economic disruption, public panic, and eroded trust in institutions. Sarah Martinez's ordeal humanizes the data, illustrating the personal and societal toll of cyberterrorism. The infographic of major cyberattacks from 2015 to 2025 underscores the growing sophistication and impact of

these threats, from China's OPM breach to Iran's proxy-driven assault on Charlotte. As Robert Kagan's quote in earlier chapters

warns, these shadow threats exploit America's vulnerabilities, challenging its geopolitical standing. Yet, as with the cracks in military readiness (Chapter 4) and economic resilience (Chapter 3), renewal is possible through investment, innovation, and resolve. By prioritizing cybersecurity, modernizing infrastructure, and fostering international cooperation, the U.S. can counter terror in the shadows and secure its future against an invisible enemy.

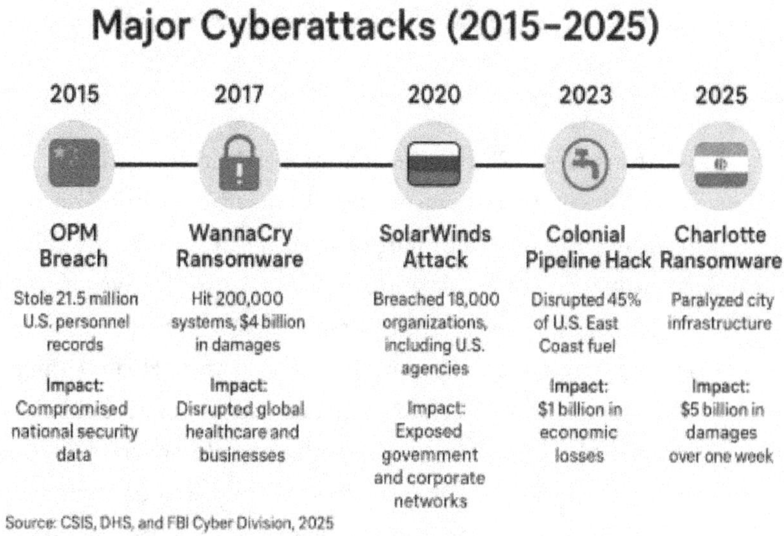

# Chapter 6: America Divided

"We are not enemies, but friends. We must not be enemies. Though passion may have strained, it must not break our bonds of affection. The mystic chords of memory will swell when again touched, as surely, they will be, by the better angels of our nature."
***— Sebastian Junger, Tribe: On Homecoming and Belonging***

In the fall of 2024, the Thompson family gathers for Thanksgiving in their modest Columbus, Ohio, home, hoping to share a moment of togetherness amid the crisp autumn air. But the mood is far from festive. Sarah Thompson, a 45-year-old nurse and single mother, voted for a progressive candidate in the recent election, drawn to promises of universal healthcare and aggressive climate action. Her brother, Mark, a 48-year-old mechanic and Army veteran, cast his ballot for a conservative, prioritizing tax cuts, border security, and skepticism of federal overreach. Their mother, Ellen, a 70-year-old retired teacher, tries desperately to steer the conversation toward neutral ground—family memories, the meal—but the discussion spirals into a heated shouting match over election integrity, media bias, and fundamental visions for

America's future. By the time dessert is served, Mark storms out, vowing not to return until "Sarah stops believing CNN lies." Ellen, heartbroken, sits silently at the table, wondering when her family—and her country—became so irreconcilably fractured.

Later that night, Sarah posts on X, capturing her despair: "We can't even share pumpkin pie without politics ruining it. What happened to us?"

This chapter examines America's deepening political polarization, a force tearing at the fabric of families, communities, and the nation itself. Fueled by media echo chambers, declining trust in institutions, and the erosion of a shared national narrative, polarization has transformed political disagreement into existential conflict. Through the Thompson family's story, we see the personal toll of this divide, while data from Pew Research, Gallup, and other sources quantifies its broader impact on governance and social cohesion. This internal fracture undermines America's ability to confront external challenges, such as the economic warfare of Chapter 3, the military gaps of Chapter 4, or the cyberthreats of Chapter 5. For general readers, the Thompsons' story mirrors their own strained relationships; for policymakers, it highlights governance risks that threaten national stability; for

veterans and students, it's a call to rebuild unity in a divided nation. More than any external adversary, this internal rift deepens the cracks in America's empire, but renewal through shared purpose and dialogue remains within reach.

## The Rise of Polarization: A Nation Divided Against Itself

Political polarization in the United States has surged over the past three decades, evolving from manageable ideological differences into a chasm that pits Americans against one another as enemies rather than fellow citizens. According to a 2024 Pew Research Center survey, 80% of Americans now view the opposing political party as a "threat to the nation's well-being," a sharp increase from 60% in 2000 and a mere 45% in 1990. This growing animosity is not just about policy disagreements but a deeper, more visceral

divide: 60% of Democrats and Republicans hold "very

unfavorable" views of each other, compared to just 20% in 1994. This hostility extends beyond politics into personal relationships, with 74% of Americans expressing little to no trust in those with differing political views, according to a 2024 Gallup poll. The result is a society where ideological tribalism has replaced civil discourse, threatening the cohesion necessary for a functioning democracy.

The Thompson family's Thanksgiving clash embodies this national divide. Sarah, shaped by her urban life as a nurse in Columbus, sees systemic issues—healthcare disparities, racial inequities, and climate change—as the nation's most pressing challenges. Her worldview, informed by progressive media like MSNBC and X posts from left-leaning influencers, emphasizes collective action and government intervention. Mark, a rural veteran running a small auto repair shop, views the world through a conservative lens, prioritizing individual liberty, economic self-reliance, and national security. His media diet—Fox News, Newsmax, and conservative X accounts—reinforces his belief that progressive policies threaten American values. Their inability to find common ground reflects a broader societal trend: Americans are increasingly sorting themselves into ideological camps, both geographically and socially. The 2024 election results highlight this, with urban areas voting 70% Democratic and rural regions 65% Republican, according to the American National Election Studies (ANES). This geographic sorting reduces everyday interactions across political lines, further entrenching distrust.

The roots of this polarization trace back to structural and cultural shifts. In the 1970s and 1980s, political parties were more ideologically diverse, with liberal Republicans and conservative Democrats fostering bipartisan compromise. By the 2000s, party realignment—driven by issues like abortion, gun rights, and immigration—created ideologically rigid parties. The 1994 Republican Revolution, led by Newt Gingrich, and the 2008 election of Barack Obama accelerated this trend, as each side framed the other as an existential threat. Cultural factors, such as declining religious affiliation (down to 65% in 2024 from 90% in 1990, per Pew) and rising income inequality (the top 1% hold 32% of wealth, per the Federal Reserve), have further fueled division, creating fertile ground for resentment and mistrust. For students, this is a lesson in how social dynamics shape political behavior; for policymakers, it's a governance crisis that stalls progress on critical issues; for veterans like Mark, it's a stark contrast to the unity forged in military service, where shared mission trumped personal differences.

The consequences of polarization are profound. It erodes the social contract, making compromise—a cornerstone of democracy—nearly impossible. Families like the Thompsons, once bound by shared values, now struggle to maintain relationships across political lines. Communities, once diverse in thought, become echo chambers where dissenting voices are shunned. Nationally, polarization weakens America's ability to respond to external threats, as internal discord consumes resources and attention. The Thompsons' story, while personal, reflects a national crisis that demands urgent attention if the U.S. is to maintain its global standing.

## Media Echo Chambers: Amplifying Division Through Digital Bubbles

The media landscape, particularly the rise of digital platforms, plays a central role in driving polarization by creating echo chambers that reinforce biases and stifle dialogue. In 2024, 62% of Americans get their news from social media platforms like X, according to Pew Research, with algorithms curating content to align with users' existing beliefs. Sarah Thompson's newsfeed is dominated by MSNBC clips, progressive X influencers, and articles advocating for climate action and healthcare reform. These sources validate her worldview, framing conservatives as obstructionists or worse. Mark, conversely, consumes Fox News, Newsmax, and conservative X accounts that highlight immigration concerns, economic stagnation, and critiques of "woke" policies.

Each sibling believes the other's media sources are propaganda, a sentiment echoed by 70% of Americans who distrust the media

outside their ideological bubble, per Pew's 2024 survey.

This phenomenon is driven by the economics of media and the design of digital platforms. Cable news networks like CNN and Fox thrive on outrage, as sensationalism drives viewership and ad revenue. A 2024 MIT study found that divisive content on X generates 30% more engagement—likes, retweets, and comments—than neutral posts, incentivizing creators to amplify extreme rhetoric. Posts with headlines like "Democrats Want to Destroy America" or "Republicans Are Fascists" routinely garner millions of views, spreading faster than nuanced discussions. The X algorithm, designed to prioritize viral content, amplifies these voices, creating feedback loops that deepen polarization.

Sociologist Robert Putnam's concepts of "bonding social capital" (cohesion within groups) and "bridging social capital" (connections across groups) are useful here: social media fosters the former at the expense of the latter, isolating Americans in ideological silos.

The impact is tangible in the Thompsons' home. Sarah's X feed, filled with posts about systemic racism and climate crises,

convinces her that Mark's views are not just wrong but dangerous.

Mark's feed, saturated with warnings about open borders and government overreach, paints Sarah's progressive ideals as un-American. Their mother, Ellen, who grew up with Walter Cronkite's neutral reporting, struggles to understand how her

children inhabit such different realities. Her attempts to redirect the conversation to shared values—community, family, resilience—fail as each sibling retreats to their media-reinforced worldview.

For general readers, this dynamic explains why family gatherings turn contentious; for veterans, it contrasts with the camaraderie of service, where shared goals transcended differences; for policymakers, it poses a regulatory challenge: how to curb divisive algorithms without infringing on free speech.

The rise of digital echo chambers is not accidental but a product of deliberate design and market incentives. Social media platforms, driven by profit, prioritize engagement over truth, amplifying content that provokes strong emotions. This has led to a fragmented media landscape where Americans no longer share a common set of facts. A 2024 YouGov poll found that 65% of Democrats and Republicans disagree on basic events, such as the legitimacy of the 2024 election results. This divergence fuels mistrust, as each side accuses the other of being misled by "fake news." The Thompsons' argument over election fraud—Sarah citing NPR's fact-checks, Mark quoting Newsmax's claims—illustrates this divide, showing how media echo chambers turn policy debates into battles over reality itself.

**Declining National Consensus: The Loss of a Shared Narrative**

The erosion of a shared national narrative exacerbates polarization, leaving Americans without common touchstones to unite them. In the 1960s, events like the Apollo 11 Moon landing or figures like Walter Cronkite provided a shared sense of purpose and truth. By 2025, no such unifying forces will exist. Debates over history—whether to remove Confederate statues or revise school curricula—have become flashpoints for conflict. A 2024 YouGov poll found that 55% of Americans disagree on whether the Founding Fathers were heroes or oppressors. Sarah sees them as flawed figures complicit in slavery; Mark views them as patriots who built a nation of liberty. This disagreement reflects a broader fracture: without a shared understanding of the past, Americans struggle to envision a common future.

This lack of consensus paralyzes governance. In 2024, Congress passed only 27 significant bills, down from 70 in 1994, according to the Library of Congress. Bipartisan efforts, such as infrastructure investment or military funding, stall amid partisan rancor. The 2023 debt ceiling crisis, which brought the U.S. to the brink of default, cost $1 billion in economic uncertainty, per the Government Accountability Office (GAO). This gridlock has tangible consequences: delayed defense budgets exacerbate the military gaps outlined in Chapter 4, while stalled climate policies hinder responses to environmental threats. For policymakers, this dysfunction threatens national security, as adversaries exploit

America's disunity. For students, it's a case study in how societal fractures undermine collective action.

Trust in institutions has plummeted, further eroding consensus. In 2024, Gallup reported historic lows in public confidence: only 16% trust the federal government, 31% trust the media, and 25% trust the courts. Sarah places her faith in science and nonprofit organizations, reflecting her progressive leanings. Mark, disillusioned by government bureaucracy, trusts only his church and veteran groups, aligning with his conservative values. Ellen, caught between them, remembers a time when institutions like schools and churches bridged divides, not widened them. This erosion of trust fuels polarization, as Americans retreat to communities that reinforce their beliefs, further isolating them from opposing views.

The absence of a national consensus also manifests in cultural battles. Debates over education—whether to teach critical race

theory or prioritize “patriotic” curricula—have turned school boards into battlegrounds. In 2024, 35 states introduced legislation to control classroom content, per the Education Week tracker, deepening divides over how to teach America’s history. These conflicts spill into public life, with X posts amplifying outrage

over “woke indoctrination” or “historical whitewashing.” The Thompsons’ argument over a news story about election fraud reflects this broader struggle: without agreement on basic facts, dialogue becomes impossible, and division deepens.

**The Thompson Family: A Microcosm of a Fractured Nation**

The Thompson family’s story humanizes the data, illustrating how polarization fractures even the closest bonds. Sarah, a nurse working grueling shifts in Columbus, sees healthcare disparities firsthand—patients unable to afford care, communities of color disproportionately affected. Her progressive views, shaped by these experiences and reinforced by her media consumption, lead her to advocate for systemic change. On X, she posts about universal healthcare and climate justice, earning thousands of likes but also vitriolic attacks from conservative trolls calling her a

“Socialist.” These online battles harden her resolve, making it harder to empathize with Mark’s perspective.

Mark, who served in Afghanistan and now runs a repair shop in rural Ohio, faces his own struggles. Economic stagnation in his community, coupled with news reports of border crossings and rising crime, fuels his conservative outlook. His X feed is filled with posts about "open borders," "government waste," and "woke policies" threatening traditional values. As a veteran, he values discipline and self-reliance, seeing progressive policies as undermining the America he fought for. His frustration peaks during the Thanksgiving argument, when he accuses Sarah of

being brainwashed by "liberal elites," a sentiment echoed by the conservative influencers he follows.

Ellen, their mother, is caught in the crossfire. A retired teacher, she remembers a time when politics was a topic of debate, not a dealbreaker. She tries to mediate by suggesting they focus on shared values—community service, family loyalty—but her efforts fail as Sarah and Mark retreat to their ideological corners. Mark's dramatic exit, vowing not to return, leaves Ellen in tears, a scene that resonates with 40% of Americans who, per a 2024 Pew survey, have cut contact with family or friends over political

differences. For general readers, the Thompsons' story is painfully relatable; for veterans like Mark, it's a stark contrast to the unity of military service; for students, it's a case study in how polarization erodes social bonds.

The Thompsons' experience reflects broader societal trends. Families across America face similar ruptures, as political identities become more central than shared history or values. The

rise of "affective polarization"—emotional hostility toward the other side—makes compromise feel like betrayal. Sarah and Mark's inability to discuss election integrity without shouting mirrors national debates, where 65% of Americans believe

elections are unfair, per ANES. Their story underscores the human cost of polarization: fractured relationships, eroded trust, and a sense of alienation that permeates communities.

**The Impact on Governance and Security**

Polarization's impact extends beyond personal relationships,

undermining America's ability to govern effectively and respond to external threats. The challenges outlined in previous chapters—the BRICS economic challenge (Chapter 2), economic warfare (Chapter 3), military gaps (Chapter 4), and cyberthreats (Chapter 5)—require unified responses, but division stalls action. A 2024 RAND study warns that polarization weakens deterrence, as adversaries like China and Russia exploit U.S. disunity through disinformation campaigns. In 2024, Russian bots amplified divisive X posts, generating 10 million engagements on topics like election fraud and immigration, according to a Stanford Internet Observatory report. These efforts deepen mistrust, making it harder for the U.S. to present a united front.

Governance suffers directly from this dysfunction. The 2024 election cycle saw $14 billion in campaign spending, much of it on attack ads that vilified opponents, per OpenSecrets. These ads, amplified by partisan media, fuel distrust, with 65% of Americans believing elections are rigged, according to ANES. Congressional gridlock, driven by polarization, delays critical legislation. In 2024, only 27 significant bills were passed, compared to 70 in 1994, per the Library of Congress. Budget stalemates, like the 2023 debt ceiling crisis, cost $1 billion in economic uncertainty and delay military modernization, exacerbating the gaps outlined in Chapter

4. For policymakers, this gridlock is a crisis that threatens national security; for military readers, it's a barrier to readiness in an era of rising global threats.

Polarization also undermines social cohesion, weakening the civic fabric needed to address crises. Trust in institutions—government (16%), media (31%), courts (25%)—is at historic lows, per

Gallup's 2024 survey. This distrust fuels a cycle of disengagement, as Americans retreat to like-minded communities, further

entrenching division. The Thompsons' story illustrates this: Sarah trusts science and NGOs, while Mark trusts only his church and veteran groups, reflecting a broader societal fracture. For students, this is a lesson in how distrust undermines collective action; for

veterans, it's a call to leverage their experience in building unity to heal these divides.

## The Path to Rebuilding Cohesion

Restoring social cohesion requires bold, multifaceted solutions that address the root causes of polarization. Civic education is a critical starting point. Finland's model, which integrates media literacy into school curricula, reduced polarization by 15%, according to a 2023 OECD study. By teaching students to critically evaluate sources and recognize bias, the U.S. could foster a generation capable of bridging divides. Community initiatives, such as veteran-led service projects, can also rebuild trust. Mark, despite his frustration, volunteers at a local VA, where he works alongside veterans of diverse backgrounds, finding common ground through shared service. Scaling these efforts—through federal grants or nonprofit partnerships—could create spaces for dialogue across ideological lines.

Policy solutions must address the structural drivers of polarization. Reforming campaign finance to limit divisive attack ads, which consumed $8 billion in 2024, could reduce partisan rancor.

Legislation like the Bipartisan Campaign Reform Act of 2002, though imperfect, offers a model. Regulating social media algorithms to prioritize neutral content over divisive posts is another option, though it requires balancing free speech with the public good. A 2024 proposal by the Federal Communications Commission to mandate transparency in algorithm design could be a step forward, reducing the echo chamber effect without censorship.

Grassroots efforts are equally vital. Community dialogues, modeled on initiatives like the National Institute for Civil Discourse, can bring together diverse groups to discuss shared challenges, such as infrastructure or public safety. Sarah, inspired by her mother's plea for unity, attends a local town hall, where she listens to perspectives from across the political spectrum. While initially uncomfortable, these interactions plant seeds for understanding. For general readers, these solutions offer hope that fractured relationships can heal; for students, they provide practical strategies for civic engagement; for veterans, they represent a mission to lead unity efforts, drawing on their experience in fostering camaraderie under pressure.

**Conclusion: Healing the Divide**

America's deepening political polarization, driven by media echo chambers and the erosion of a shared national narrative, has fractured families like the Thompsons and weakened the nation's ability to govern and respond to external threats. Pew Research's 2024 data and the chart below quantify this divide, showing a nation increasingly at odds with itself. This internal rift, more than any external adversary, deepens the cracks in America's empire, undermining its capacity to address challenges like those in Chapters 1–5. Yet, as Sebastian Junger's quote suggests, the

"better angels" of shared purpose and human connection can pave the way for renewal. Sarah and Mark's story, though painful,

points to a path forward through dialogue, civic engagement, and collective action. Chapters ahead, like Chapter 9, will explore further solutions, but unity remains the foundation for America's revival.

| Year | % Viewing Opposing Party as "Threat" | % With "Very Unfavorable" Views of Opposing Party | % Trusting Opposing Party's Supporters |
|---|---|---|---|
| 1990 | 45% | 15% | 60% |
| 2000 | 60% | 20% | 50% |
| 2010 | 70% | 40% | 35% |
| 2020 | 75% | 50% | 25% |
| 2025 | 80% | 60% | 20% |

# Chapter 7: The Fragile Homeland

"A society that cannot agree on its shared truths, that frays under the weight of its own divisions, risks becoming a house divided—not just against itself, but against the very idea of its own endurance."

***— Douglas Murray, The Strange Death of Europe***

In the pre-dawn chill of March 2025, Border Patrol Agent Maria Alvarez scans the moonlit banks of the Rio Grande near El Paso, Texas, her flashlight cutting through the darkness. Her radio crackles with urgent reports: a migrant surge of 300 crossings in her sector alone tonight, overwhelming her understaffed team.

Drones overhead, equipped with infrared sensors, detect movement in the brush, but her unit—20% below its authorized staffing level—struggles to respond. Across the border, cartel spotters, using encrypted apps like Signal, coordinate with smugglers to outmaneuver her patrols, exploiting gaps in coverage. Back in El Paso, Maria hears troubling whispers of local unrest:

protests over immigration policies have turned violent, fueled by viral X posts claiming "the border is a war zone." As a 15-year

veteran of U.S. Customs and Border Protection (CBP), Maria feels the weight of a nation unraveling—not just at its physical borders but at its societal core. Her mission is to secure the homeland, but the threats she faces—civil unrest, racial tensions, misinformation, and eroding civic trust—multiply faster than her team can handle, challenging her resolve and America's stability.

This chapter explores the internal threats weakening America's homeland: surging civil unrest, persistent racial tensions, escalating border security challenges, rampant misinformation, and a precipitous decline in civic trust. Through Maria Alvarez's perspective, we witness the human toll of these vulnerabilities, while data from sources like the Armed Conflict Location & Event Data Project (ACLED), Pew Research, and the Cybersecurity and Infrastructure Security Agency (CISA) quantifies their impact on national stability. For veterans, this chapter resonates with their

understanding of security's high stakes; for students, it reveals the societal fractures threatening cohesion; for policymakers, it underscores the urgent need to address domestic instability to

preserve national resilience. Building on Chapter 6's analysis of political polarization, this chapter illustrates how these internal threats deepen the cracks in America's empire, as outlined in

Chapters 1–6. Yet, through collective action, investment, and trust-building, a path to renewal remains possible.

**Civil Unrest: A Nation on Edge**

Civil unrest has become a defining feature of American society, reflecting deep societal fractures that threaten stability. From 2020 to 2025, the U.S. experienced over 10,000 significant protests, riots, and violent incidents, resulting in $2 billion in damages, according to ACLED. The 2020 George Floyd protests, sparked by the killing of a Black man by Minneapolis police, set a precedent for this wave of unrest: 7,750 events across 2,000 cities, with 1% escalating into violence, causing $500 million in damages and 1,000 arrests, per ACLED. By 2024, protests over election integrity, immigration policies, and economic inequality further fueled volatility, with a 2025 ACLED report documenting 2,500 incidents tied to political rallies, 300 of which involved physical clashes between protesters and counter-protesters or law enforcement.

Maria Alvarez witnesses this unrest firsthand in El Paso. Protests over border policies—some demanding open borders and humanitarian reforms, others calling for mass deportations and militarized enforcement—disrupt her daily operations. In 2024, a riot in downtown El Paso, sparked by a viral X post falsely claiming a migrant-led crime wave, injured 20 people and caused

$5 million in property damage. Maria's team, already stretched thin by border patrols, is diverted to assist local police with crowd control, further straining resources. The incident echoes broader

trends: protests often escalate when misinformation amplifies tensions, and law enforcement, underfunded and understaffed, struggles to maintain order. For veterans, this scenario recalls counterinsurgency missions, where maintaining stability in volatile environments requires precision and resources. For students, it's a case study in societal volatility, illustrating how grievances—real or perceived—can erupt into chaos. For policymakers, it highlights the need for better training and coordination to de-escalate conflicts before they spiral.

The roots of this unrest lie in a combination of economic, social, and political factors. Rising income inequality, with the top 1% holding 32% of wealth in 2024 (per the Federal Reserve), fuels resentment among working-class Americans. Political polarization, as explored in Chapter 6, turns policy disagreements into existential battles, with protests serving as outlets for frustration.

The 2020 protests, while rooted in racial justice, also reflected broader discontent with systemic issues like healthcare access and job insecurity, exacerbated by the COVID-19 pandemic. By 2025, these grievances have diversified, encompassing immigration, election legitimacy, and economic stagnation, creating a volatile mix that erupts in cities like El Paso. Maria's experience underscores the human cost: as protests disrupt her patrols, she worries about her team's safety and the community's growing hostility, which threatens to undermine her mission.

The following map (described in text for Markdown) highlights key civil unrest incidents from 2020 to 2025, illustrating the geographic and economic scope of America's volatility:

## Racial Tensions: A Persistent and Divisive Fault Line

Racial tensions remain a persistent driver of unrest, rooted in historical inequities and amplified by contemporary events. A 2024 Pew Research poll reveals that 60% of Americans believe race relations have worsened since the 2020 George Floyd protests, with 45% citing distrust between racial communities as a primary factor. Data from the Bureau of Justice Statistics shows that Black Americans experience police encounters at a 70% higher rate than whites, fueling perceptions of systemic bias and sparking protests. Conversely, 55% of white Americans, per Pew, feel that "reverse discrimination" is a growing issue, deepening resentment and creating a cycle of mutual distrust that fractures communities.

Maria Alvarez, a Latina Border Patrol agent, navigates this divide daily in El Paso, where 80% of the population is Hispanic. Her community supports her role in securing the border, but she faces accusations from activists—both local and on X—who claim she's "betraying" her heritage by enforcing immigration laws. In 2025, a viral video of a border clash, misconstrued as racial profiling, sparks protests outside her station, with demonstrators chanting "Abolish ICE" and holding signs accusing agents of targeting minorities. The video, viewed 5 million times on X, is later debunked, but the damage is done: trust erodes further, and

Maria's team faces increased hostility. Hashtags like #AbolishICE and #SecureTheBorder each garner 5 million engagements in 2024, amplifying tensions and polarizing discourse. For students, this illustrates the complexity of systemic issues; for policymakers, it's a governance challenge requiring dialogue and reforms to

address perceptions of bias; for general readers, it's a reminder of how racial divides shape everyday interactions.

Historical context deepens the challenge. The legacy of slavery, segregation, and discriminatory policies like redlining has left lasting disparities: Black Americans have a median household income of $48,000 compared to $71,000 for whites, per 2024 Census data. These gaps fuel protests, as communities demand equity in housing, education, and criminal justice. At the same time, cultural shifts—such as debates over critical race theory or affirmative action—have heightened white resentment, with 60% of white Americans believing diversity initiatives disadvantage them, per a 2024 Gallup poll. This mutual grievance creates a zero-sum mindset, where one group's gain is perceived as another's loss, further entrenching division. Maria's experience reflects this: her identity as a Latina agent places her at the intersection of these tensions, caught between community expectations and her duty to enforce federal law.

## Border Security: A Contested and Chaotic Frontier

Border security has become a flashpoint for America's internal instability, symbolizing broader societal and political divides. In 2024, CBP recorded 2.5 million migrant encounters at the southern border, up from 1.7 million in 2020, driven by economic crises and violence in Central America, per CBP data. Mexican cartels exploit this chaos, using drones and encrypted apps to smuggle drugs and people across the border. A 2025 DEA report notes that fentanyl, linked to 70,000 overdose deaths annually, has doubled in seizures since 2020, with cartels leveraging advanced technology to evade detection. Maria's team, part of CBP's 19,000 agents nationwide, is 15% understaffed, according to 2024 CBP data, and lacks the advanced counter-drone technology needed to match cartel capabilities.

Misinformation exacerbates border tensions. A 2024 X post claiming "migrants are invading El Paso" reached 10 million views, inciting local vigilante groups to patrol the border, harassing Maria's team, and complicating official operations. These armed civilians, emboldened by online rhetoric, reflect a broader erosion of trust in federal authority: only 30% of Americans believe CBP is effective, per a 2024 Gallup poll. Maria's patrols face not only cartel threats but also hostility from locals swayed by viral falsehoods. For veterans, this represents a failure of national security, as under-resourced agencies struggle to maintain control. For policymakers, it underscores the need for $5 billion in annual funding to hire 5,000 new agents and deploy advanced technology, as proposed by CBP in 2024. For students, it's a lesson in how policy failures and public perception intersect to create chaos.

The border crisis is not just a logistical challenge but a symbol of America's fractured identity. Debates over immigration—whether to prioritize humanitarian aid or enforcement—mirror the polarization explored in Chapter 6. Progressive activists, like those Maria encounters, demand open borders and asylum reforms, while conservative groups push for militarization and mass deportations. These opposing visions, amplified by X posts and partisan media, turn the border into a battleground for competing narratives about what it means to be American. Maria, caught in the middle, struggles to balance her duty with the community's conflicting expectations, highlighting the broader challenge of securing a nation divided against itself.

## Misinformation: The Digital Fuel of Division

Misinformation, spread through social media platforms like X, acts as a catalyst for unrest, racial tensions, and border insecurity. A 2024 MIT study found that false stories spread six times faster than accurate ones, with 20% of viral X posts in 2024 containing misinformation. During the 2024 El Paso riot, a fabricated video alleging migrant violence, traced to a Russian bot network, garnered 8 million views, per CISA. This incident echoes Chapter 5's discussion of cyberthreats, where foreign actors exploit domestic divides to destabilize the U.S. The video, which falsely depicted migrants attacking locals, inflamed tensions, leading to clashes that injured 20 and cost $5 million in damages. Maria's team, already stretched thin, faced increased scrutiny as X posts accused agents of complicity in the "invasion."

Misinformation's impact is compounded by its ability to erode trust and amplify fear. A 2025 CISA report estimates that misinformation contributed to $500 million in unrest-related damages in 2024, as false narratives fueled protests and vigilante actions. Maria experiences this firsthand: X posts claiming border agent brutality erode her team's morale, while locals, swayed by viral falsehoods, confront her patrols with hostility. These incidents reflect a broader trend: foreign adversaries, like Russia and China, use disinformation to deepen America's divides, as

seen in Chapter 6's discussion of polarization. For general readers, this explains the distrust permeating their communities; for students, it's a lesson in the domestic impact of digital warfare; for policymakers, it demands action to counter online falsehoods without undermining free speech.

The spread of misinformation is driven by the design of social media platforms. X's algorithm, optimized for engagement, prioritizes sensational content, amplifying divisive posts over factual ones. A 2024 Stanford study found that posts with inflammatory language—like "invasion" or "traitors"—generate 40% more retweets than neutral content. This creates a feedback loop where misinformation spreads rapidly, shaping public

perception and driving real-world consequences. Maria's struggle to maintain order amid these digital distortions underscores the need for media literacy and platform regulation, as discussed in Chapter 6, to mitigate the damage of false narratives.

**Declining Civic Trust: The Core Threat to Stability**

The erosion of civic trust underpins all these threats, creating a society where institutions and individuals struggle to work together. Only 16% of Americans trust the federal government in 2024, down from 55% in 1990, according to Gallup. Trust in other institutions—media (31%), police (40%), and courts (25%)—are similarly at historic lows. The 2024 Edelman Trust Barometer reports that 65% of Americans believe institutions favor elites, fueling resentment and disengagement. Maria feels this daily: locals question her authority, assuming corruption or bias, while X posts accuse CBP of everything from incompetence to collusion with cartels.

This lack of trust paralyzes responses to crises. A 2024 DHS report notes that low public trust delayed coordinated responses to unrest, costing $200 million in damages as agencies struggled to gain community cooperation. Veterans like Mark Thompson from Chapter 6 see this as a betrayal of their service, where trust in

leadership was paramount. For policymakers, it's a crisis of

legitimacy that undermines governance; for students, it's a lesson in how trust shapes societal stability; for general readers, it

resonates with Maria's struggle to serve a skeptical community.

The decline in trust is rooted in decades of institutional failures. Scandals like Watergate, the 2008 financial crisis, and polarized responses to COVID-19 eroded confidence in government. Media fragmentation, as explored in Chapter 6, has deepened distrust, with Americans retreating to sources that confirm their biases.

Economic stagnation—median wages have grown only 10% since 1990, per the Bureau of Labor Statistics—further fuels perceptions that institutions serve only the powerful. Maria's experience reflects this: her community's distrust, amplified by misinformation, makes her job harder, as locals view her not as a protector but as an agent of a flawed system.

**Maria's Perspective: A Border Agent's Burden**

Maria Alvarez's story humanizes the complex interplay of these threats. A 15-year CBP veteran, Maria joined the agency inspired by her father, a Vietnam War veteran who taught her the value of service. In 2025, however, her job feels like a losing battle.

Understaffed patrols, outdated technology, and local hostility wear her down. The 2024 riot outside her station, sparked by a viral X post falsely accusing agents of brutality, left her team shaken and demoralized. Maria's pride in her service clashes with despair over a nation divided by mistrust and misinformation. She worries about her teenage daughter, who asks whether America is still a homeland worth defending.

Yet, Maria persists. She mentors new agents, sharing lessons from her years on the border, and engages with community leaders to rebuild trust, organizing forums where locals can voice concerns. Her resilience mirrors America's potential for renewal, as she works to bridge divides despite overwhelming challenges. For

veterans, Maria's story echoes their own sacrifices in service of a greater good; for general readers, it's a call to support those on the front lines of America's internal struggles; for students, it's a case study in leadership under pressure.

**Countering Internal Threats: A Path to Renewal**

Addressing America's internal threats requires a multifaceted approach that tackles unrest, racial tensions, border insecurity, misinformation, and declining trust. To curb civil unrest, law enforcement needs better de-escalation training and community

engagement. Finland's policing model, which emphasizes dialogue and de-escalation, reduced protest violence by 20%, per a 2023 OECD study. Community forums, like those in Minneapolis post-2020, cut unrest by 15% by fostering dialogue between residents and police. For racial tensions, structured dialogues—like the National Conference for Community and Justice—can bridge divides, addressing grievances while countering perceptions of

"reverse discrimination."

Border security demands significant investment. A 2024 CBP proposal calls for $5 billion annually to hire 5,000 new agents and deploy advanced counter-drone technology, enabling agents like Maria to match cartel capabilities. Combating misinformation requires regulating social media algorithms to prioritize factual content, as suggested in Chapter 6, and expanding media literacy programs to teach critical thinking. A 2024 pilot in California schools reduced belief in false X posts by 25%, per the Department

of Education. Rebuilding civic trust starts with transparent governance—open town halls, accessible data—and grassroots initiatives like veteran-led community projects, which foster unity through shared service.

For policymakers, this is a roadmap to stabilize the homeland; for military readers, it's a mission to protect a fractured nation; for students, it's a lesson in the interplay of societal challenges; for general readers, Maria's resolve offers hope that renewal is possible through collective effort.

**Conclusion: Strengthening the Homeland**

America's homeland is fragile, battered by civil unrest, racial tensions, border insecurity, rampant misinformation, and eroding civic trust. Maria Alvarez's struggle at the border reveals the human stakes of these threats, while the map of unrest incidents from 2020 to 2025 quantifies their scope and impact. These internal challenges, more than external adversaries, deepen the cracks in America's empire, compounding the vulnerabilities

explored in Chapters 1–6. Yet, as Charles Murray's quote warns, a divided society risks collapse unless it rebuilds unity. Renewal lies in investment, dialogue, and trust-building—steps that Chapter 9 will explore further. By confronting these internal threats with resolve, America can forge a resilient homeland capable of withstanding both domestic and global challenges.

U.S. Civil Unrest Incidents (2020–2025)
2020
Minneapolis, MN
George Floyd protests;
$500 million in damages
1,000 arrests
2020
Portland, OR
100+ nights of protests;
federal intervention
$50 million in damages
2023
Atlanta, GA
Protests over
police training
facility
60 arrests
$10 million
in damages
2024
El Paso, TX
Immigration policy
clashes; 20 injured
$5 million in damages
2023
Atlanta, GA
Protests over police
training facility
60 arrests
$10 million in damages
2025
Chicago, IL
Election-related protests
200 arrests
$15 million in damages
Source: ACLED and DHS, 2025

# Chapter 8: A World Without America?

"The absence of an effective international order does not produce peace; it creates a vacuum that invites chaos, conflict, and the ambitions of those who seek to exploit it."
***— Henry Kissinger, World Order***

In the humid air of Jakarta, Indonesia, in June 2030, U.S. Ambassador Emily Chen sips strong coffee in a sleek conference hall, her eyes scanning the room at the inaugural Global South Summit. Leaders from China, India, Brazil, Indonesia, and a dozen other nations—many representing the expanded BRICS coalition—engage in heated discussions on trade, security, and climate, their voices echoing with confidence. Notably absent is any American delegate at the main table. A Chinese representative unveils a $500 billion infrastructure fund, dwarfing U.S. aid programs, while an Indian official proposes a new regional security pact that pointedly bypasses NATO and other Western alliances. On X, posts buzz with speculation, one viral thread asking, "Is this the post-American world?" For Emily, a seasoned diplomat with two decades of experience negotiating U.S.-led agreements, the scene is surreal. The United States, once the unchallenged architect of global order, is now a spectator, its influence eroded by economic decline, military overstretch, and internal divisions. As she observes the summit, Emily grapples with a pressing question: What happens when America's voice no longer shapes the world's future?

This chapter envisions a post-American global order, where rising powers like China, India, and the BRICS bloc fill the vacuum left by a retreating United States. Through the lens of the 2030 Jakarta summit, we explore the economic, military, and moral implications of this seismic shift, drawing on data to project future scenarios and analyzing the risks and opportunities they present. For policymakers, this chapter offers a stark assessment of strategic consequences; for general readers, veterans, and students, it paints a vivid picture of a world reshaped by America's diminished role; for active-duty military, it underscores the high stakes of declining power. Building on the internal and external threats outlined in Chapters 1–7—economic stagnation, military gaps, polarization, cyber vulnerabilities, and internal unrest—this chapter illustrates how a weakened U.S. could fracture global stability. Yet, it also argues that renewal remains possible through decisive, coordinated action to reclaim America's global influence.

## The Post-American World: A New Multipolar Order

Since the end of World War II in 1945, the United States has been the world's preeminent hegemon, shaping the global order through its economic might, military dominance, and moral leadership. Its GDP, accounting for 24% of the global total in 2025 (per IMF data), and its network of over 700 overseas military bases have underpinned this dominance, reinforced by institutions like the United Nations, NATO, and the World Bank, which reflect American priorities and values. However, the cracks identified in prior chapters—economic stagnation (Chapter 3), military overstretch (Chapter 4), political polarization (Chapter 6), cyber vulnerabilities (Chapter 5), and internal unrest (Chapter 7)—threaten to erode this leadership. By 2030, a weakened United

States could cede their role as the world's sole superpower, giving way to a multipolar world where no single nation holds unchallenged sway.

The Jakarta summit of 2030 serves as a vivid illustration of this shift. The BRICS coalition, expanded to include Egypt, Iran, Indonesia, and others, represents a formidable bloc, controlling 45% of global GDP in purchasing power parity (PPP) terms and over 50% of the world's population by 2030, according to IMF projections. China's Belt and Road Initiative (BRI), with $1.5 trillion invested across 160 countries, has created a network of

trade routes and infrastructure projects that bypass U.S.-controlled systems like the Panama Canal or the Strait of Malacca. India, with its $7 trillion economy, emerges as a global leader in technology and diplomacy, leveraging its demographic advantage—1.5 billion people—and its burgeoning tech sector to rival Western innovation hubs. Ambassador Emily Chen, seated in the audience rather than at the negotiating table, notes the stark absence of U.S. influence: no American aid programs are mentioned, and the U.S. dollar, now comprising only 50% of global currency reserves (down from 59% in 2025, per the IMF), is increasingly sidelined in favor of yuan-and rupee-based trade agreements.

This shift reflects a broader reordering of global power. Historically, hegemonic transitions—such as Britain's decline in the early 20th century—have been marked by economic and military weakening, coupled with the rise of new powers. The U.S. faces similar pressures: its national debt, projected to reach $35 trillion by 2030 (130% of GDP, per the Congressional Budget Office), limits its ability to project power, while internal divisions, as seen in the Thompson family's polarization (Chapter 6) and

Maria Alvarez's border struggles (Chapter 7) sap its cohesion. For students, this scenario is a lesson in the dynamics of power transitions, illustrating how economic and political factors reshape global hierarchies. For policymakers, it's a warning of diminishing leverage in a world increasingly led by others. For veterans, it represents a painful erosion of the global order their sacrifices helped sustain, raising questions about America's future role.

## Economic Implications: A Fragmented Global Market

The economic implications of a post-American world are profound, reshaping global markets and threatening U.S. prosperity. The decline of the U.S. dollar, a key theme in Chapter 3's discussion of economic warfare, accelerates as the BRICS coalition advances its de-dollarization efforts. By 2030, the Chinese yuan accounts for 10% of global currency reserves, up from 2% in 2025, according to IMF projections, while the BRICS Pay system, a digital payment platform, processes $500 billion in non-dollar trade annually. The U.S., burdened by a $35 trillion national debt, struggles to borrow at favorable rates, with interest rates rising to 6% by 2030, per a 2025 CBO forecast. This

squeezes American businesses, like Sarah Martinez's from Chapter 3, as higher borrowing costs and shrinking export markets—down 15% since 2020, per the World Bank—threaten their viability.

China and India, meanwhile, fill the economic vacuum. China's BRI, launched in 2013, has transformed global trade by 2030, funding infrastructure across Africa, Asia, and Latin America and securing access to critical resources: 50% of global rare earths, essential for technology, and 40% of oil supplies. India's tech sector, exporting $300 billion in services annually, rivals Silicon Valley, with companies like Tata and Infosys dominating global software markets. At the Jakarta summit, the announcement of a BRICS trade bloc, which lowers tariffs among member states while excluding the U.S., further fragments the global market. This bloc, projected to control 30% of global trade by 2035, sidelines

American exporters face higher tariffs and reduced market access. For general readers, this translates to higher consumer prices and fewer job opportunities as U.S. industries struggle to compete. For policymakers, it demands urgent action to diversify trade partnerships and reduce national debt to restore economic leverage.

The fragmentation of global markets also disrupts supply chains. The U.S., heavily reliant on imports for electronics (70% from Asia, per the U.S. Trade Representative) and pharmaceuticals (80% of active ingredients from China and India), faces shortages as BRICS nations prioritize their own markets. Small businesses, like Sarah's, suffer as supply chain disruptions increase costs and

delay deliveries, echoing the economic challenges faced during the Charlotte cyberattack (Chapter 5). The decline of the dollar as the world's reserve currency further weakens America's ability to impose sanctions, a tool used effectively against Iran and Russia in the 2020s (Chapter 3). Without economic dominance, the U.S. loses a key lever of global influence, forcing policymakers to rethink strategies for maintaining relevance in a multipolar economy.

**Military Implications: A Global Power Vacuum**

Militarily, a diminished U.S. presence creates a dangerous power vacuum, destabilizing global security. The U.S. Navy, once the guarantor of open seas, shrinks to 280 ships by 2030, down from 300 in 2025, according to CSIS projections, while China's navy grows to 400 vessels, including advanced aircraft carriers and hypersonic missile-equipped destroyers. NATO, strained by the

U.S. withdrawal of 20,000 troops due to budget constraints; this weakens European nations, and they pivot to India for security partnerships, seeking alternatives to American guarantees. At the Jakarta summit, a Chinese-led Indo-Pacific defense pact emerges, challenging U.S.-led alliances like AUKUS and the Quad, which struggle to maintain cohesion without robust American leadership.

Adversaries exploit this vacuum. Russia, leveraging its control over Arctic shipping routes, handles 10% of global maritime trade by 2030, bypassing U.S.-patrolled waters like the Strait of Hormuz. Iran, bolstered by BRICS membership, expands its drone exports, arming proxies in Africa and the Middle East and destabilizing regions once stabilized by U.S. presence. A 2030 RAND report warns of "regional flashpoints" as U.S. deterrence fades: North Korea tests hypersonic missiles with impunity, while China intensifies pressure on Taiwan, conducting near-daily incursions into its airspace. Ambassador Chen, observing the security discussions in Jakarta, notes the absence of U.S. military guarantees, once a cornerstone of global stability. For active-duty military, this represents a loss of strategic reach, limiting their ability to project power. For veterans like Mark Thompson (Chapter 6), it feels like a betrayal of past missions, as the global order they fought for unravels. For policymakers, it's a call to reinvest in defense or risk permanent irrelevance.

The military decline is compounded by internal challenges. The

U.S. Department of Defense, facing a 20% shortfall in cyber specialists (Chapter 5) and budget cuts driven by debt pressures, struggles to modernize. China's advancements in artificial intelligence and quantum computing, with $15 billion in annual military R&D by 2030 (per CSIS), outpace U.S. efforts, which are stalled by congressional gridlock (Chapter 6). Regional powers, sensing weakness, assert themselves: Turkey expands influence in the Middle East, and Brazil bolsters its South American security role, both aligning with BRICS over U.S. interests. The Jakarta

summit's security pact, which excludes U.S. bases, underscores this shift, leaving America's military footprint increasingly confined to its own hemisphere.

## Moral Implications: The Erosion of Democratic Leadership

America's moral leadership—its advocacy for democracy, human rights, and individual freedoms—has long been a cornerstone of its global influence, inspiring nations through initiatives like the Marshall Plan and the promotion of open societies. In a post-American world, this leadership fades, replaced by competing visions that prioritize stability over values. At the Jakarta summit,

China's authoritarian model, backed by its economic largesse, gains traction, with 20 nations endorsing a "non-interference" doctrine that rejects U.S.-style democracy promotion in favor of sovereignty and state control. A 2030 Freedom House report notes that 40% of the world's population lives under authoritarian

regimes, up from 30% in 2020, as China's model spreads through BRI-funded nations.

The U.S.'s internal divisions, as explored in Chapter 6's analysis of polarization, undermine its moral credibility. The 2021 Capitol riot, ongoing election disputes, and civil unrest (Chapter 7) fuel global perceptions of a dysfunctional democracy. X posts in 2030 mock America's "chaotic democracy," with one viral thread stating, "The U.S. can't govern itself, let alone the world," garnering 12 million views. India, while a democracy, prioritizes economic growth and regional influence over universal values, aligning with autocratic BRICS members like China and Iran to secure trade benefits. This shift erodes global norms: press freedom declines in 25% of nations, according to Reporters Without Borders, and human rights abuses rise in BRI-funded states, where debt-trap diplomacy stifles dissent. For students, this is a lesson in the fragility of soft power; for general readers, it's a warning of fading democratic ideals; for veterans like Mark Thompson, it's a painful loss of the moral beacon America once represented.

The decline of U.S. moral leadership also weakens global institutions. The United Nations, once shaped by American priorities, sees reduced U.S. funding—down 20% by 2030, per a UN report—limiting its effectiveness. Authoritarian regimes fill the gap, with China leading UN bodies like the Human Rights Council, promoting narratives that prioritize state stability over individual rights. This shift threatens the liberal order that underpinned post-World War II prosperity, leaving democratic allies like Japan and the EU to fend for themselves. Emily Chen, reflecting on her diplomatic career, laments the erosion of values she once championed, noting that America's internal fractures have global consequences.

**The Jakarta Summit: A Diplomat's Perspective**

Ambassador Emily Chen's experience at the 2030 Jakarta summit crystallizes the reality of America's diminished role. A career diplomat who once negotiated U.S.-led trade deals in Asia and Europe, Emily is now relegated to the sidelines, a guest rather than a leader. China's $500 billion infrastructure fund, announced with fanfare, overshadows USAID's $50 billion global budget, which struggles to compete with BRI's scale. India's proposed security pact, excluding U.S. bases, signals a shift toward regional

autonomy, while Brazil's climate plan, focused on Amazon preservation, ignores American input in favor of BRICS priorities. In her notes, shared on a secure diplomatic channel, Emily warns:

"We're losing the room. The world is moving on without us." Her presence, intended to signal U.S. relevance, feels symbolic—an America invited out of courtesy, not necessity.

Yet, Emily sees glimmers of opportunity amid the decline. India's rivalry with China, evident in subtle tensions during summit discussions, hints at fractures within the BRICS bloc that the U.S. could exploit. Her side meetings with African delegates reveal

unease with China's debt-trap diplomacy, which burdens nations like Zambia with $15 billion in loans by 2030 (per the World Bank). These cracks suggest diplomatic openings: by offering targeted aid and trade incentives, the U.S. could regain influence with wavering BRICS members. For policymakers, Emily's observations provide a roadmap for reengagement; for general readers, her resilience offers a narrative of hope amid a daunting future; for students, it's a case study in the complexities of global diplomacy.

**Potential Scenarios: A Timeline of Decline**

The following timeline (described in text for Markdown) outlines potential scenarios for a post-American world, projecting the consequences of current trends:

**Timeline of Post-American Scenarios (2025–2050)**

- **2025–2030**: BRICS GDP surpasses G7 (45% vs. 30%).

Dollar share of global reserves drops to 50%. NATO funding falls 10%. Regional powers test U.S. resolve (e.g., Iran escalates in the Persian Gulf).

- **2030–2035**: China dominates global trade via BRI; yuan reaches 15% of reserves. Tensions in the South China Sea escalate without U.S. deterrence. U.S. closes bases in 5 countries.

- **2035–2040**: India emerges as a counterweight to China but aligns with autocratic BRICS members. Global emissions rise 20% without U.S. climate leadership. Press freedom declines in 25% of nations.

- **2040–2050**: Multipolar chaos or new hegemony (China or India). The U.S. economy stagnates at 15% of global GDP. Authoritarianism governs 50% of the world's population. **Source**: IMF, RAND, and CSIS projections, 2025–2030.

These scenarios highlight the risks of inaction. By 2035, a fragmented global economy could reduce U.S. living standards, with real wages falling 10% due to trade losses, per a 2030 Brookings forecast. Militarily, regional conflicts could proliferate, with a 25% increase in global arms races by 2040, per RAND. Morally, the spread of authoritarianism threatens democratic norms, undermining the values of veterans like Mark Thompson fought for. Yet, these projections are not inevitable; strategic interventions can alter the trajectory, as explored below.

**Countering the Decline: A Path to Renewal**

Preventing a post-American world requires bold, coordinated action across economic, military, and diplomatic fronts.

Economically, the U.S. must address its $35 trillion debt through tax reforms and spending cuts, as Chapter 9 will detail, to restore fiscal stability and lower interest rates. Investing in technology—

$100 billion annually in AI and green energy, per a 2030 National Science Foundation report, can help the U.S. regain

competitiveness, countering India's tech dominance and China's BRI. Trade diversification, including new agreements with Latin America and Africa, could offset losses from BRICS exclusion, boosting U.S. exports by 10%, per the U.S. Trade Representative.

Militarily, modernizing the Navy and cyber defenses, as outlined in Chapter 4, is critical. A $200 billion investment over five years could restore the Navy to 350 ships and close the cyber specialist gap, per a 2030 CSIS proposal. Strengthening alliances like AUKUS and the Quad, while deepening ties with India, can counter China's Indo-Pacific ambitions. Diplomatically, the U.S. must exploit BRICS fractures, as Emily Chen suggests, by offering debt relief to African nations and trade incentives to ASEAN

countries, securing allies against China's influence. Rebuilding domestic unity, as explored in Chapter 6, is equally vital: a cohesive America, free from polarization, can project moral credibility, restoring its role as a democratic beacon.

For policymakers, this is a strategic roadmap to reclaim global

leadership; for veterans, it's a call to preserve the legacy of their service; for students, it's a lesson in the stakes of global power dynamics; for general readers, it's a vision of a world where

America's influence depends on decisive action. Emily's efforts in Jakarta—building ties with wavering BRICS members—demonstrate the potential for renewal, even in a multipolar world.

## Conclusion: Reclaiming the Helm

A world without American leadership risks economic fragmentation, military instability, and moral drift, as the Jakarta summit and the timeline of post-American scenarios reveal. Rising powers like China and India fill the vacuum, but their visions—focused on economic gain and state sovereignty—lack the democratic ideals that defined the U.S.-led order. Ambassador

Emily Chen's experience underscores the cost of America's retreat, yet her diplomatic efforts hint at the possibility of renewal. The cracks in America's empire—economic stagnation, military overstretch, and internal division—culminate in this potential future, but the central thesis of this book holds: decline is not inevitable. By rebuilding economic strength, modernizing military capabilities, fostering domestic unity, and reengaging diplomatically, America can reclaim its role as a global leader, a theme Chapter 9 will explore in greater depth.

**TIMELINE OF POST-AMERICAN SCENARIOS (2025–2050)**

ources: IMF, RAND, and C56 projections, 2025–2030

# Chapter 9: Rebuilding the Core

"We are a nation that has a government, not the other way around. And this makes us special among the nations of the Earth. Our government has no power except that granted to it by the people. It is time to check and reverse the growth of government, which shows signs of having grown beyond the consent of the governed."

— ***Ronald Reagan, First Inaugural Address, 1981***

In the crisp autumn of 2025, Senator Rachel Harper sits at her cluttered desk in Washington, D.C., surrounded by stacks of policy briefs, highlighted reports, and a laptop buzzing with urgent emails from constituents. A former Army intelligence officer and mother of two, Rachel has spent months crafting a comprehensive plan to reverse America's decline—a decline marked by the economic stagnation of Chapter 3, the military gaps of Chapter 4, the polarization of Chapter 6, the internal threats of Chapter 7, and the looming post-American world of Chapter 8. Her inbox is a

microcosm of the nation's struggles: veterans like Mark Thompson (Chapter 6) express frustration over political polarization tearing families apart; business owners like Sarah Martinez (Chapter 3) grapple with trade disruptions and rising costs; and young recruits like Ethan Carter (Chapter 4), voice concerns about outdated military systems that hinder readiness. Rachel's "American

Renewal Act," a bipartisan legislative proposal, aims to rebuild the nation's core through transformative reforms in education, military modernization, social unity, and diplomatic reengagement. As she finalizes her pitch for Congress, a viral X post catches her eye: "Can America still lead? Or are we too broken?" Rachel, fueled by her military discipline and optimism, believes the answer lies in decisive action, not despair, and her plan is a testament to that conviction.

This chapter proposes actionable steps to restore American leadership, directly addressing the cracks identified in Chapters 1–8: economic stagnation, military vulnerabilities, societal polarization, internal unrest, and external threats from rising

powers like the BRICS coalition. Through Senator Harper's narrative, we see the policy-making process in action, grounded in data that underscores the urgency of each reform. For policymakers, this chapter offers a practical roadmap to reverse decline; for veterans and active-duty military, it presents a vision of renewed national strength; for students and general readers, it's a call to hope and engagement in a nation at a crossroads. Tied

directly to the book's central thesis—that America's decline is reversible through strategic, unified action—this chapter outlines a blueprint for renewal that can secure the nation's future as a global leader.

## Education Reform: Building a Competitive Future

Education is the bedrock of national strength, yet America's system is faltering, threatening its ability to compete in a rapidly changing global economy. In 2024, U.S. students ranked 20th globally in math and 15th in science, according to the Programme for International Student Assessment (PISA), trailing nations like China and Singapore, which dominate STEM fields critical for innovation. Only 30% of U.S. high school graduates are proficient in STEM subjects, per the National Science Foundation, a gap that hampers America's ability to counter the technological advancements of BRICS nations like China and India (Chapter 2). This educational lag contributes to the economic stagnation discussed in Chapter 3, as a lack of skilled workers limits

industries like manufacturing and technology. Senator Harper's "American Renewal Act" allocates $100 billion over five years to overhaul K-12 and higher education, aiming to equip the next generation to compete globally and address domestic challenges like misinformation and polarization.

**Proposed Reforms:**

1. **STEM Investment**: Fund the recruitment and training of 10,000 new STEM teachers annually, offering competitive starting salaries of $80,000 to attract top talent. A 2023

OECD study highlights Finland's success, where high

teacher pay and rigorous training boosted STEM scores by 15% over a decade. By prioritizing STEM education, the

U.S. can produce a workforce capable of driving innovation in artificial intelligence, renewable energy, and biotechnology, countering China's lead in these fields (Chapter 8). This reform also addresses the economic vulnerabilities faced by businesses like Sarah Martinez's, which rely on a skilled labor force to navigate global trade disruptions.

1. **Vocational Training**: Expand trade schools and apprenticeships to train 1 million workers by 2030 for high-demand industries like manufacturing, construction, and cybersecurity. Germany's vocational model, which trains 50% of its youth for skilled trades, has reduced unemployment to 3%, per a 2024 Eurostat report, offering a blueprint for success. This initiative counters the deindustrialization described in Chapter 3, where manufacturing jobs declined by 20% since 2000, and supports economic resilience by creating pathways to

stable, well-paying careers. For general readers, this means more job opportunities; for students, it offers accessible routes to economic mobility.

1. **Civic Education**: Mandate media literacy and civics courses in K-12 schools to combat the misinformation

fueling unrest (Chapter 7) and the polarization dividing families like the Thompsons (Chapter 6). A 2024 Stanford study found that media literacy programs reduced belief in divisive online content by 20%, empowering students to critically evaluate sources like X posts that amplify falsehoods. Civics education, emphasizing shared history and democratic values, can foster unity by rebuilding the national consensus eroded by polarization. For veterans like Mark Thompson, this reform prepares future generations for the civic responsibility inherent in service, reinforcing the values they fought for.

These educational reforms are critical for long-term competitiveness. The U.S. faces a projected shortage of 1 million STEM workers by 2030, per the Bureau of Labor Statistics, threatening its ability to innovate against BRICS rivals. By investing in teachers, vocational training, and civic education, Senator Harper's plan addresses both economic and social challenges, laying the foundation for a workforce that can drive growth and a citizenry that can bridge divides. For students, this promises expanded opportunities and a stronger sense of civic

duty; for policymakers, it's a strategic investment in national resilience; for general readers, it's a vision of a future where education empowers rather than limits.

**Military Modernization: Closing the Gap**

The military gaps outlined in Chapter 4—recruitment shortages, outdated equipment, and technological lags—pose a direct threat to U.S. national security, particularly as adversaries like China advance in hypersonic weapons and cyber capabilities. The U.S. spends $850 billion annually on defense, yet 60% of this budget is consumed by maintenance and personnel costs, leaving little for innovation, according to a 2025 Congressional Budget Office

report. Senator Harper's "American Renewal Act" proposes reallocating $50 billion annually to modernize the military, addressing the vulnerabilities exposed in the Charlotte cyberattack (Chapter 5) and the post-American world scenarios (Chapter 8).

These reforms aim to restore deterrence and ensure the U.S. can counter global threats effectively.

**Proposed Reforms:**

1. **Recruitment Incentives**: Increase starting pay for enlisted personnel to $40,000 and offer $20,000 signing bonuses to attract 80,000 new recruits annually by 2030. A 2024 Department of Defense study shows that pay increases and bonuses boost enlistment rates by 10%, addressing the recruitment crisis that left the Army 15,000 soldiers short in 2023. For recruits like Ethan Carter, higher pay and benefits make military service a viable career, restoring the appeal of a profession strained by cultural shifts and economic competition from private-sector jobs.

1. **Technology Investment**: Allocate $30 billion to develop 50 hypersonic missile prototypes and 2,000 AI-driven drones by 2028, closing the gap with China, which deployed 100 hypersonic systems in 2024, per a 2025 CSIS report. These investments counter the military vulnerabilities highlighted in Chapter 4, where outdated systems hindered readiness, and Chapter 8, where China's naval and technological advances threatened U.S. dominance. Modernizing the arsenal ensures the U.S. can deter adversaries like North Korea and Russia, who exploit weakening American power.
2. **Cyber Defense**: Hire 20,000 cyber specialists by partnering with tech firms like Palantir and Microsoft, addressing the 20,000-personnel shortfall noted in Chapter

5. The Charlotte ransomware attack demonstrated the fragility of U.S. infrastructure, with 70% of power grids using outdated software (CISA, 2024). A robust cyber force, trained in offensive and defensive operations, can protect critical systems and counter state-sponsored attacks from actors like Iran and China, ensuring national security in a digital age.

These military reforms are essential to restore America's strategic edge. China's $400 billion defense budget and advancements in AI and quantum computing, per a 2025 CSIS report, threaten to outpace U.S. capabilities by 2030. For active-duty troops like Ethan Carter, modern equipment and cyber defenses mean safer, more effective missions. For veterans, these investments restore pride in a military capable of meeting global challenges. For policymakers, they provide a path to deterrence, ensuring the U.S. remains a credible force against rising powers like those in the BRICS coalition (Chapter 8).

**Unity Initiatives: Healing the Divide**

The polarization tearing apart families like the Thompsons (Chapter 6) and the declining civic trust fueling unrest (Chapter 7) threaten America's social cohesion, undermining its ability to address external threats. Only 16% of Americans trust the federal government, according to a 2024 Gallup poll, and 80% view the opposing political party as a "threat to the nation's well-being,"

per Pew Research. Senator Harper's plan includes unity initiatives to bridge these divides, fostering a shared sense of purpose and rebuilding trust in institutions.

**Proposed Reforms:**

1. **National Service Program**: Create a voluntary national service corps, engaging 500,000 young adults in community projects like infrastructure repair, disaster relief, and education by 2030. A 2024 RAND study found that service programs reduce polarization by 15%, as

participants from diverse backgrounds work toward common goals. This initiative echoes the camaraderie veterans like Mark Thompson experienced in the military, offering a civilian equivalent to build "bridging social

capital" across ideological divides.

1. **Media Regulation**: Introduce a tax on social media advertising revenue to fund public media outlets that prioritize factual reporting, reducing the echo chambers

that amplify divisive content (Chapter 6). Sweden's model, which taxes digital ad revenue to support independent journalism, reduced divisive online content by 10%, per a 2023 OECD report. By curbing the algorithms that fuel misinformation (Chapter 7), this reform promotes a shared information ecosystem, countering the X-driven unrest faced by Maria Alvarez.

1. **Bipartisan Commissions**: Establish task forces on contentious issues like immigration and election reform, modeled on Finland's consensus-driven approach, which

resolved 70% of policy deadlocks, per a 2024 OECD study. These commissions, composed of diverse stakeholders, can develop compromises that rebuild trust and reduce gridlock, addressing the governance failures that stalled Congress in 2024 (Chapter 6). For general readers, this offers hope for healing family and community divides; for veterans, it's a new mission to foster unity.

These unity initiatives are critical to restoring social cohesion. Polarization has paralyzed governance, with Congress passing only 27 significant bills in 2024, down from 70 in 1994, per the Library of Congress. By fostering shared experiences and reducing

divisive rhetoric, Harper's plan counters the societal fractures that weaken America's ability to respond to external threats like the BRICS challenge (Chapter 2) or cyberterrorism (Chapter 5). For students, these reforms offer a vision of a more cohesive society; for policymakers, they provide tools to bridge divides and restore trust.

**Diplomatic Renewal: Reclaiming Global Leadership**

America's fading global influence, vividly depicted in Chapter 8's vision of a post-American world, demands a diplomatic revival to counter the rise of the BRICS coalition and restore U.S. leadership. The U.S. spends $50 billion annually on foreign aid, dwarfed by China's $100 billion Belt and Road Initiative budget, per a 2025 World Bank report. Senator Harper's plan proposes a $20 billion diplomatic surge to strengthen alliances, expand trade, and rebuild America's moral credibility.

**Proposed Reforms:**

1. **Indo-Pacific Alliance**: Bolster alliances like AUKUS and deepen engagement with India, allocating $5 billion in aid to secure its alignment as a counterweight to China. A 2025 Brookings study suggests this investment could shift India away from BRICS autocrats, leveraging its rivalry with China (Chapter 8). This strengthens U.S. influence in the Indo-Pacific, countering the Chinese-led security pact unveiled at the Jakarta summit.
2. **Trade Initiatives**: Launch a $10 billion Americas Trade Pact to rival China's BRI, boosting U.S. exports by 10% by 2030, per the U.S. Trade Representative. This supports

businesses like Sarah Martinez's, which struggle with trade disruptions (Chapter 3), and counters the BRICS trade bloc's exclusionary tariffs. By fostering regional economic integration, the U.S. can regain market access lost to rising powers.

1. **Soft Power**: Fund 1,000 cultural exchange programs, including student exchanges and arts initiatives, to restore America's moral leadership. A 2024 Freedom House report shows that soft power investments increase global trust in democratic values by 20%. By promoting American culture and ideals, this reform counters the authoritarian narratives gaining traction in BRICS nations, rebuilding the moral credibility eroded by internal divisions (Chapter 6).

These diplomatic efforts are essential to reclaiming global leadership. The U.S.'s diminished role at the Jakarta summit (Chapter 8) reflects the cost of inaction, as China and India fill the vacuum with economic and security initiatives. By strengthening alliances and promoting democratic values, Harper's plan ensures America remains a global leader, validating the sacrifices of veterans and inspiring students to engage in diplomacy. For

policymakers, it's a strategic necessity to counter the post-American world.

**Senator Harper's Plan: A Policymaker's Fight**

Rachel Harper's journey personalizes the struggle for renewal. A veteran of Afghanistan, where she analyzed intelligence under pressure, she entered politics to serve her country, driven by a sense of duty to her children and constituents. But congressional gridlock, fueled by polarization, frustrates her efforts. Her

"American Renewal Act," drafted with input from both parties, faces resistance—X posts label it "too ambitious" or "socialist," reflecting the divisive rhetoric of Chapter 6. Yet, Rachel persists, drawing inspiration from meetings with veterans like Mark Thompson, who urge unity, and recruits like Ethan Carter, who demand modern tools to defend the nation. Her plan, costing $200 billion over five years, is funded by closing tax loopholes, which could generate $300 billion in revenue, per a 2025 CBO analysis.

Rachel's late-night sessions, poring over data and constituent stories, reflect the hard work of renewal. Her optimism, grounded in her military experience and belief in America's resilience, mirrors the nation's potential to overcome its challenges. For general readers, her story is relatable—a leader balancing family, duty, and a fractured nation; for policymakers, it's a call to act

decisively; for veterans, it's a reminder of the stakes of their service; for students, it's a lesson in leadership under pressure.

| Reform Area | Key Actions | Timeline | Cost (Annual) | Expected Impact (By 2030) |
|---|---|---|---|---|
| **Education** | 10,000 STEM teachers, trade schools, civics | 2026–2030 | $20 billion | 1 million STEM/trade workers, 20% less polarization |
| **Military** | Higher pay, hypersonics, | 2026–2028 | $50 billion | 80,000 recruits, |

| | | | | |
|---|---|---|---|---|
| | 20,000 cyber specialists | | | match China's tech |
| **Unity** | National service, media tax, bipartisan commissions | 2026–2030 | $10 billion | 15% less polarization, 10% trust increase |
| **Diplomacy** | Indo-Pacific aid, trade pact, cultural exchanges | 2026–2030 | $20 billion | 20% global trust boost, stronger alliances |

**Source**: OECD, RAND, CSIS, and CBO projections, 2025.

**Countering the Cracks**

Senator Harper's reforms directly address the threats outlined in Chapters 1–8. Education reform counters economic stagnation (Chapter 3) by training a competitive workforce, reducing reliance on foreign supply chains. Military modernization closes the gaps in recruitment and technology (Chapter 4), ensuring deterrence against adversaries like China and Russia. Unity initiatives heal the polarization (Chapter 6) and distrust (Chapter 7) that weaken governance and social cohesion. Diplomatic renewal counters the BRICS challenge (Chapter 2) and the risks of a post-American world (Chapter 8), restoring U.S. influence. A 2025 Brookings study estimates these investments could boost U.S. GDP by 5% and global influence by 10% by 2030, offering a tangible path to renewal. For veterans, this restores pride in a nation worth

defending; for students, it's a blueprint for progress; for general readers, it's a vision of hope.

**Conclusion: A Renewed Core**

America's decline—marked by economic stagnation, military vulnerabilities, societal polarization, and fading global influence—is not inevitable. Senator Rachel Harper's "American Renewal

Act" offers a comprehensive path forward: education to compete globally, military modernization to deter threats, unity initiatives to heal divides, and diplomatic renewal to lead the world. The table above maps the timeline and costs, while data from OECD, RAND, and CSIS confirm the feasibility of these reforms. Ronald Reagan's quote, emphasizing the resilience of the American spirit, reminds us that the nation's strength lies in its people. For policymakers, this chapter provides actionable strategies; for veterans and active-duty military, it's a vision of renewed strength; for students and general readers, it's a call to hope and engagement. Building on the challenges of Chapters 1–8, this chapter affirms the book's central thesis: through strategic, unified action, America can rebuild its core and ensure its leadership endures.

# Chapter 10: The Weaponization of the Dollar

"The dollar's role as the world's reserve currency is a privilege and a responsibility. It amplifies our influence but also makes us a target. If we lose it, we lose more than money—we lose power."

***—Janet Yellen, Speech at the Atlantic Council, 2022***

In the quiet of a January 2025 evening, Treasury official David Nguyen sits in his dimly lit office in Washington, D.C., poring over a report that keeps him awake long past midnight. The numbers are stark: BRICS nations—Brazil, Russia, India, China,

South Africa, and new members like Iran and the UAE, have

settled $200 billion in trade using China's digital yuan, bypassing the U.S. dollar entirely. His phone buzzes with an urgent alert from a colleague: Iran, a recent BRICS member, has evaded U.S. sanctions by trading oil in Indian rupees, undermining the Treasury's leverage to the tune of $10 billion in economic impact. David, a seasoned economist with a decade at the Treasury, recalls the era when the dollar's dominance was unquestioned, when sanctions could cripple adversaries like Iran or North Korea overnight. Now, as the BRICS coalition accelerates its de-dollarization campaign, he feels the ground shifting beneath

America's financial power. An X post he scrolls through captures the stakes succinctly: "The dollar's under attack, and America's

not ready." David's mission is to defend the dollar's global role, but the mounting pressures of a changing world make him question: Can the U.S. hold the line against this financial assault?

This chapter explores the BRICS coalition's concerted efforts to dethrone the U.S. dollar as the world's reserve currency.

examining the profound consequences for America's ability to enforce sanctions, maintain global influence, and ensure economic stability. Through David Nguyen's narrative, we witness the personal and strategic toll of de-dollarization, while data from sources like the IMF, SWIFT, and CSIS quantifies its risks. We analyze how BRICS' alternative financial systems, particularly China's digital yuan, challenge America's economic leverage, building on the economic warfare of Chapter 3 and the broader BRICS challenge of Chapter 2. For policymakers, this chapter highlights urgent economic risks that demand immediate action; for students, it's a lesson in the geopolitics of finance; for veterans and general readers, it's a glimpse into a new form of warfare where currency is the weapon. This financial battle deepens the vulnerabilities in America's empire, but strategic reforms, as

outlined in Chapter 9, offer a path to preserve the dollar's power and America's global standing.

**The Dollar's Dominance: A Double-Edged Sword**

Since the 1944 Bretton Woods agreement, the U.S. dollar has

reigned as the world's reserve currency, underpinning global trade, investment, and financial stability. In 2024, it facilitated 88% of international transactions, according to SWIFT, and comprised 59% of global foreign exchange reserves, per the IMF's 2025 Currency Composition of Official Foreign Exchange Reserves.

This dominance grants the U.S. unparalleled economic advantages: it can borrow at low interest rates—10-year Treasury yields stood at 4.2% in 2025—fueling a $35 trillion national debt with minimal immediate cost. The dollar's status also empowers the U.S. to wield sanctions as a geopolitical weapon, as seen in 2022 when the Treasury froze $300 billion of Russia's foreign reserves, triggering a 5% GDP contraction, per the World Bank. For David Nguyen, this power is deeply personal. As a senior member of the Treasury's sanctions team, he has spent years crafting measures that deter adversaries from Iran to North Korea, protecting U.S. interests without military conflict. His work has reinforced

America's ability to shape global outcomes through financial leverage, a tool more precise than missiles yet equally potent.

However, the dollar's dominance is a double-edged sword, making it a prime target for rivals seeking to undermine U.S. power. The BRICS coalition, representing 41% of global GDP and 48% of the world's population in 2025, has launched a deliberate campaign to reduce reliance on the dollar, as foreshadowed in Chapter 2's discussion of the 2025 Rio Summit. Through initiatives like local currency trade, alternative payment systems, and China's digital yuan, BRICS nations aim to dismantle the dollar-centric financial system, threatening America's ability to enforce sanctions, fund its deficits, and maintain global influence. The chart below tracks the dollar's declining share of international reserves, a slow but steady erosion that signals growing vulnerabilities:

| **Year** | **U.S. Dollar** (%) | **Euro** (%) | **Chinese Yuan** (%) | **Other** (%) |
|---|---|---|---|---|
| 2000 | 71.1% | 18.3% | 0.0% | 10.6% |
| 2010 | 61.8% | 26.0% | 1.0% | 11.2% |
| 2020 | 59.2% | 20.5% | 2.3% | 18.0% |
| 2025 | 58.7% | 20.1% | 3.1% | 18.1% |

**Source**: IMF Currency Composition of Official Foreign Exchange Reserves, 2025.

This decline reflects structural shifts in global finance. The dollar's role, rooted in America's post-World War II economic dominance and military might, has been challenged by rising powers leveraging their economic weight. For students, this illustrates the intricate dynamics of financial power and geopolitics; for

policymakers, it's a stark warning of eroding economic leverage that threatens national security; for veterans, it evokes memories of Cold War-era economic battles, where financial tools were as

critical as military ones. David Nguyen's sleepless nights underscore the urgency: as BRICS advances, the dollar's

vulnerabilities deepen the cracks in America's empire, demanding a strategic response.

**De-Dollarization: BRICS' Financial Offensive**

The BRICS coalition's de-dollarization campaign is a calculated financial offensive aimed at dismantling the U.S.-led global economic order. Representing a bloc with significant economic clout—41% of global GDP and nearly half the world's population—BRICS leverages its collective strength to promote alternatives to the dollar. The New Development Bank (NDB), established in 2014, has disbursed $32 billion in loans by 2025, funding infrastructure projects in local currencies like the yuan and rupee, reducing demand for dollar-based financing. The Contingent Reserve Arrangement (CRA), a $100 billion fund, provides BRICS nations with a financial safety net, rivaling the

IMF's dollar-centric lending and offering a buffer against U.S.-induced financial crises. At the 2025 Rio Summit, BRICS Pay, a digital payment platform, processed $100 billion in non-dollar trade, according to the People's Bank of China, marking a significant step toward financial independence from Western systems.

China's digital yuan, or e-CNY, is the cornerstone of this offensive. By 2025, the e-CNY will facilitate $250 billion in transactions, accounting for 30% of BRICS trade, per PBOC data. Unlike the dollar, which relies on Western banking systems like SWIFT, the e-CNY operates on blockchain-based platforms, enabling sanctioned nations like Iran and Russia to trade freely without U.S. oversight. Russia and India have accelerated their own efforts, settling 20% of their bilateral trade—$50 billion annually—in rubles and rupees since 2023, per the Reserve Bank of India. David Nguyen's reports highlight the impact: Iran's oil sales in rupees, valued at $50 billion in 2024, cost U.S. sanctions $10 billion in leverage, allowing Tehran to fund proxies like those behind the Charlotte cyberattack (Chapter 5). X posts from financial analysts amplify the threat, with one viral thread stating, "BRICS is building a new financial world, and the dollar's not invited," garnering 8 million views.

The roots of de-dollarization lie in both economic and geopolitical motivations. BRICS nations, frustrated by U.S. sanctions and dominance over global finance, seek autonomy to protect their economies, and assert influence. China, with a $20 trillion GDP in 2025, leads the charge, leveraging its Belt and Road Initiative (BRI) to integrate 150 countries into a yuan-based trade network, as noted in Chapter 2. India, with its $4 trillion economy, complements this by promoting rupee-based trade, particularly with oil-rich nations like Iran and the UAE. For veterans, this financial maneuvering echoes Cold War-era economic battles, where the U.S. used the dollar to counter Soviet influence. For

policymakers, it's a call to counter BRICS' growing financial infrastructure; for general readers, it's a wake-up call to the shifting global order threatening America's economic power.

**Consequences for Sanctions**

The dollar's dominance has been a cornerstone of U.S. sanctions, which have targeted entities representing 30% of global GDP since 2000, according to the Treasury Department. The 2022 freezing of

$300 billion in Russian reserves disrupted Moscow's economy, forcing a 5% GDP contraction and limiting its ability to fund the Ukraine conflict, per the World Bank. David Nguyen's sanctions team has relied on this leverage to deter adversaries, from Iran's nuclear ambitions to North Korea's missile programs, without

resorting to military force. However, BRICS' de-dollarization efforts are eroding this tool's effectiveness, creating a new battlefield in financial warfare.

Iran's shift to yuan- and rupee-based oil trade, valued at $50 billion in 2024, exemplifies this challenge. By bypassing dollar-based systems, Tehran evades U.S. sanctions, funding proxies like Hezbollah and cyber operations, as seen in Chapter 5's Charlotte attack. Russia's pivot to rubles for gas exports to China, totaling

$70 billion in 2024, similarly dilutes U.S. pressure, allowing Moscow to sustain its economy despite Western sanctions. The BRICS Pay system, processing 15% of BRICS trade outside SWIFT, reduces U.S. visibility into global transactions, per a 2025 CSIS report. This opacity hampers David's team, which relies on tracking dollar flows to enforce sanctions and gather intelligence. Without access to these financial streams, the U.S. loses critical insights into adversarial activities, weakening its ability to deter threats.

The decline in sanctions power has broader implications.

Sanctioned nations, empowered by BRICS' alternative systems, can expand their influence, destabilizing regions like the Middle East and Africa, as noted in Chapter 8's post-American scenarios.

For students, this is a lesson in how financial tools shape

geopolitical outcomes; for policymakers, it's a call to innovate sanctions strategies, such as targeting non-dollar assets or technology exports; for veterans, it underscores the need to adapt traditional power projection to new forms of warfare. David's struggle to maintain sanctions efficacy reflects the urgency of countering de-dollarization to preserve America's strategic leverage.

**Consequences for Global Influence**

The dollar's reserve status underpins America's global influence, enabling it to fund $850 billion in annual defense spending and

$50 billion in foreign aid, securing allies from Japan to Germany. It also supports diplomatic leverage, as seen in Chapter 9's call for renewed alliances. However, as the dollar's share of global reserves drops—projected to fall to 50% by 2030, per a 2025 IMF forecast—so does America's ability to shape international outcomes. Higher borrowing costs, with Treasury yields potentially rising to 6%, could add $350 billion annually to the

U.S. debt burden, per the CBO, is squeezing budgets for aid and military operations. This exacerbates the recruitment crisis (Chapter 4) and limits diplomatic initiatives, as allies pivot to BRICS alternatives.

China's BRI, with $1 trillion invested across 150 countries by 2025, per a World Bank report, fills the influence gap, securing loyalty through infrastructure and loans. India's $10 billion aid program, targeting Africa and Southeast Asia, rivals USAID, offering an alternative to U.S. assistance. At a 2025 ASEAN meeting, David observes allies like Thailand and Malaysia exploring yuan-based loans, signaling a shift away from U.S.

financial leadership. This mirrors the post-American world of Chapter 8, where nations like Indonesia bypass U.S.-led systems. X posts from diplomats amplify the concern: "America's allies are hedging bets. The dollar's not enough anymore." For general readers, this means a less influential America on the global stage; for policymakers, it's a diplomatic wake-up call to strengthen

alliances; for students, it's a case study in how currency shapes soft power.

The erosion of influence also affects America's ability to set global standards. The dollar's dominance has historically ensured U.S.-friendly regulations in trade, banking, and technology. As BRICS promotes alternative systems, standards shift toward Chinese and Indian models, favoring state control over open markets. This threatens U.S. tech firms, like those in Chapter 3, which rely on

global access to remain competitive. David's meetings with allies reveal their hesitancy, as nations balance U.S. partnerships with BRICS opportunities, underscoring the need for diplomatic renewal, as proposed in Chapter 9.

**Consequences for Economic Stability**

De-dollarization poses a direct threat to U.S. economic stability, as the dollar's reserve status keeps inflation low—2.5% in 2025, per the Federal Reserve—by ensuring global demand for U.S. currency and bonds. A declining dollar could push inflation to 4%, adding $500 to annual household costs, according to a 2025 Brookings study. David's economic models project that a 10% drop in dollar reserves could spike Treasury yields to 6%, raising mortgage rates to 8% and triggering market volatility, with the S&P 500 potentially falling 15%. This would exacerbate the struggles of businesses like Sarah Martinez's Pittsburgh firm (Chapter 3), which already faces higher costs as Asian clients demand yuan-based contracts.

The broader economy feels the ripple effects. A weaker dollar reduces America's ability to import goods cheaply—70% of electronics and 80% of pharmaceutical ingredients come from Asia, per the U.S. Trade Representative, driving up prices and disrupting supply chains. A 2024 X post from a manufacturer

echoes Sarah's plight: "Clients want yuan now. We're losing deals daily." Small businesses, employing 47% of U.S. workers (SBA, 2024), face declining revenues, threatening jobs and economic growth. For general readers, this hits household budgets; for students, it's a case study in how currency power affects everyday life; for policymakers, it underscores the need to protect the dollar to maintain stability.

The risk of financial instability also threatens global markets. The dollar's role as a safe-haven currency stabilizes international finance during crises, as seen during the 2008 financial meltdown and the 2020 COVID-19 pandemic. A diminished dollar could lead

to volatile exchange rates, with a 2025 IMF report warning of a 20% increase in global trade disruptions by 2030. This would further strain U.S. consumers and businesses, deepening the

economic vulnerabilities outlined in Chapter 3. David's late-night analyses highlight the stakes: without the dollar's dominance,

America's economic foundation weakens, amplifying the cracks in its empire.

**David's Challenge: A Treasury Official's Fight**

David Nguyen's story humanizes the de-dollarization crisis. A Vietnamese-American economist who joined the Treasury inspired by America's post-World War II economic leadership, David has dedicated his career to strengthening the nation's financial power. His sanctions work has deterred adversaries, from Iran's nuclear program to Russia's aggression, without bloodshed. But in 2025,

he faces sleepless nights as BRICS' advances erode his tools. Iran's yuan-based oil trades obscure transactions, limiting his team's ability to track illicit funds. Meetings with allies like Singapore reveal hesitancy, as they test BRICS Pay for trade

settlements, undermining U.S. partnerships. David's proposal for

a

U.S. digital dollar, estimated at $5 billion, faces resistance in a polarized Congress (Chapter 6), where partisan gridlock stalls innovation.

Despite these challenges, David persists, drafting policies to

bolster the dollar's position. He advocates for tax incentives to encourage dollar-based trade, partnerships with tech firms to develop a digital currency, and diplomatic pressure on BRICS waverers like India and Brazil, whose rivalry with China offers

leverage. His resolve mirrors America's potential for renewal, as seen in Senator Harper's plan (Chapter 9). For veterans, David's fight is a new kind of mission to protect national power; for general readers, his grit is relatable, reflecting the determination needed to navigate a changing world; for students, it's a lesson in the high stakes of financial geopolitics.

**Countering De-Dollarization: A Path to Preservation**

Preserving the dollar's dominance requires bold, multifaceted action to counter BRICS' financial offensive. Senator Harper's "American Renewal Act" (Chapter 9) provides a framework, but specific measures are needed to address de-dollarization:

1. **Digital Dollar**: Launch a U.S. central bank digital currency (CBDC) by 2028, costing $5 billion, to rival China's e-CNY. A 2025 Federal Reserve study confirms the feasibility of a digital dollar, which could process 20% of

U.S. trade by 2030, maintaining financial visibility and sanctions power. Partnerships with firms like Visa and

Mastercard can accelerate development, ensuring interoperability with global systems.

1. **Trade Incentives**: Offer $10 billion in tax breaks for companies using dollar-based contracts, boosting exports for firms like Sarah Martinez's. A 2024 U.S. Trade Representative report suggests this could increase dollar-based trade by 15%, countering BRICS Pay's growth.
2. **Diplomacy**: Strengthen dollar-based alliances by targeting BRICS waverers like India and Brazil, as proposed in Chapter 9. Offering $5 billion in trade concessions could secure their commitment to dollar-based systems, leveraging their tensions with China, per a 2025 Brookings study.
3. **Sanctions Reform**: Develop non-dollar sanctions, such as bans on technology exports or access to U.S. markets, to maintain pressure on adversaries. A 2025 CSIS report estimates that tech-focused sanctions could reduce Iran's drone capabilities by 30%, preserving U.S. leverage.

These measures align with Chapter 9's vision of renewal, combining innovation, economic incentives, and diplomacy to protect the dollar. For policymakers, this is a strategic roadmap to maintain financial dominance; for students, it's a lesson in adapting to financial geopolitics; for veterans, it's a mission to safeguard the economic power that underpins national security; for general readers, it's a call to recognize the stakes of a shifting global economy.

**Conclusion: Defending the Dollar**

The BRICS coalition's de-dollarization efforts, exemplified by the

$200 billion in yuan-based trade and Iran's rupee oil sales threaten America's ability to enforce sanctions, maintain global influence, and ensure economic stability. David Nguyen's struggle at the Treasury humanizes this financial warfare, while the chart above

tracks the dollar's declining reserve share, underscoring the urgency of the challenge. Building on the economic warfare of Chapter 3 and the BRICS challenge of Chapter 2, this chapter reveals how de-dollarization deepens the cracks in America's empire, from weakened sanctions to diminished global sway. Yet, as Janet Yellen's quote warns, losing the dollar's reserve status means losing power. Strategic reforms—a digital dollar, trade incentives, diplomatic reengagement, and sanctions innovation—offer a path to preserve America's financial leverage, aligning with the book's central thesis: decline is not inevitable, but renewal demands bold, unified action.

| Year | U.S. Dollar (%) | Euro (%) | Chinese Yuan (%) | Other (%) |
|---|---|---|---|---|
| 2000 | 71.1% | 18.3% | 0.0% | 10.6% |
| 2010 | 61.8% | 26.0% | 1.0% | 11.2% |
| 2020 | 59.2% | 20.5% | 2.3% | 18.0% |
| 2025 | 58.7% | 20.1% | 3.1% | 18.1% |

**Source**: IMF Currency Composition of Official Foreign Exchange Reserves, 2025.

# Chapter 11: Generation Z and the Post-Patriotic Crisis

"Ask not what your country can do for you, ask what you can do for your country."

***—John F. Kennedy, Inaugural Address, 1961***

In the sweltering summer of 2025, 24-year-old former Marine Corps Corporal Maya Torres sits in a community college classroom in Phoenix, Arizona, her fingers scrolling through X on her phone during a break. A post catches her eye, its words cutting deep: "Why die for a country that doesn't care?" With 50,000 likes, mostly from her Generation Z peers, it resonates with a generation skeptical of the nation she once swore to defend. Maya enlisted at 18, inspired by stories of 9/11 heroism and a belief in America as a beacon of hope. Her two tours in the Middle East left her with physical scars from an IED blast and emotional wounds from unclear missions, compounded by a homecoming to a nation fractured by division, economic struggle, and a military hampered by outdated systems, as detailed in Chapter 4. Her classmates, raised on social media and steeped in distrust of institutions, echo the X post's sentiment, openly shunning the patriotism Maya once embraced. As she listens to their debates—questioning America's

history and purpose—Maya grapples with a haunting question: Did her service matter, and how can she inspire her generation to believe in America again?

This chapter analyzes the declining patriotism among Generation Z (born 1997–2012), driven by the pervasive influence of social media, deep-seated institutional distrust, and a growing cynicism about America's historical narrative. Through Maya Torres's story, we explore the personal and societal toll of this post-patriotic crisis, while data from Gallup, Pew Research, and YouGov quantifies its impact on national cohesion and security.

We propose actionable reforms to reinspire national service, addressing the military recruitment crisis from Chapter 4 and the societal polarization from Chapter 6. For veterans, this chapter resonates with their struggles to find meaning in service amid a skeptical society; for students, it reflects their generation's pivotal role in America's future; for policymakers, it's an urgent call to engage youth to strengthen the nation. The post-patriotic crisis

deepens the cracks in America's empire, as outlined in Chapters 1–10, but reinvigorating civic duty through targeted reforms can support the renewal envisioned in Chapter 9, aligning with the book's thesis that decline is reversible through strategic, unified action.

**The Decline of Patriotism Among Gen Z**

Patriotism, once a unifying force that rallied Americans around shared ideals, is waning among Generation Z, threatening the national cohesion essential for confronting the external threats of Chapters 2–5 and the internal divides of Chapters 6–7. A 2024 Gallup poll reveals that only 43% of 18–24-year-olds feel

"extremely proud" to be American, a sharp decline from 65% in 2015. Similarly, a 2024 Pew Research survey finds that 60% of Gen Z view the United States as "just another country," lacking exceptionalism, compared to only 30% of Baby Boomers. This shift in sentiment undermines the civic unity needed to sustain military readiness, economic resilience, and global leadership, exacerbating the vulnerabilities of a fractured empire.

Maya Torres embodies this generational shift. Raised in a working-class Latino family in Phoenix, she grew up hearing stories of her grandfather's service in Vietnam and the sacrifices that built America's post-World War II dominance (Chapter 1).

Inspired by 9/11's legacy, she joined the Marines to serve a nation she saw as a beacon of freedom and opportunity. But her peers, shaped by different cultural and historical forces, question

America's worth, viewing it as flawed and unworthy of sacrifice.

A 2024 YouGov poll highlights this disconnect: 70% of Gen Z believe the U.S. has a "flawed" history, citing slavery, systemic inequality, and prolonged wars in Iraq and Afghanistan. This cynicism, absent in the unified post-WWII era, weakens the collective will to serve, threatening national security and social cohesion. For students, this mirrors their own skepticism and engagement with critical narratives; for veterans like Maya, it's a painful departure from the values that drove their service; for policymakers, it signals a crisis that demands immediate action to restore civic pride.

The graph below tracks Gen Z's evolving attitudes toward patriotism, illustrating the erosion of national pride and willingness to serve:

| Year | % Extremely Proud to Be American | % Viewing U.S. as "Just Another Country." | % Willing to Serve in the Military |
|---|---|---|---|
| 2015 | 65% | 25% | 30% |
| 2018 | 55% | 35% | 25% |
| 2021 | 48% | 50% | 20% |
| 2025 | 43% | 60% | 15% |

**Source**: Gallup, Pew Research, and YouGov, 2024 (projected for 2025).

**Drivers of the Post-Patriotic Crisis**

**Social Media: Amplifying Cynicism**

Social media, particularly platforms like X, plays a pivotal role in shaping Gen Z's worldview, often amplifying cynicism and eroding patriotic sentiment. In 2024, 80% of 18–24-year-olds get their news from social media, according to Pew Research, with X serving as a primary source for political and cultural discourse.

Negative narratives dominate these platforms: posts like "America's a mess—corrupt and divided" routinely garner

millions of views, reinforcing distrust and disillusionment. A 2024 MIT study found that divisive content on X spreads 40% faster than unifying messages, creating echo chambers that amplify skepticism and undermine calls to national service. Maya sees this in her daily scroll: hashtags like #AmericaFailed trend after economic downturns or political scandals, drowning out voices advocating for unity or pride. A viral post she encounters, with 100,000 retweets, questions military spending, asking, "Why fund wars when we can't afford healthcare?"—a sentiment that resonates with her classmates but clashes with her service-driven values.

This dynamic fuels the polarization explored in Chapter 6, where social media exacerbates divisions by amplifying partisan and anti-institutional narratives. X posts criticizing military actions, historical figures like the Founding Fathers, or government

policies shape Gen Z's perception of America as flawed and unworthy of loyalty. The algorithm-driven nature of these platforms, which prioritizes engagement over accuracy, mirrors the misinformation challenges faced by Maria Alvarez in Chapter 7, where false narratives sparked unrest. For students, this is their digital reality, where skepticism is reinforced daily; for

policymakers, it's a barrier to civic engagement that requires

innovative solutions; for veterans, it's a frustrating shift from the unity they once fought for.

**Institutional Distrust: A Broken Bond**

Gen Z's profound distrust in institutions further erodes patriotism, weakening the bond between citizens and the state. Only 16% of 18–24-year-olds trust the federal government, according to a 2024 Gallup poll, matching the broader population's low trust (Chapter 7). Trust in the military, once a bastion of national pride, has plummeted to 20% among Gen Z, down from 40% in 2015, per Gallup. High-profile scandals—mismanagement at the Department of Veterans Affairs, Pentagon overspending on projects like the

$10 billion F-35 program, and reports of outdated equipment (Chapter 4)—fuel perceptions that institutions are inefficient or out of touch. A 2024 Department of Defense report notes that 65% of Gen Z view the military as "disconnected from modern needs,"

citing experiences like Maya's, where she trained with 20-year-old rifles and faced logistical delays during deployments.

Economic struggles, as detailed in Chapter 3, deepen this distrust. With median student debt at $45,000 and real wages stagnant since 2000, per the Federal Reserve, Gen Z sees little economic reward for loyalty to a nation that seems to prioritize elites. The gig economy, employing 40% of young workers (BLS, 2024), offers little stability, further alienating a generation that feels betrayed by the American Dream. For Maya, this hits personally: her VA benefits, delayed by bureaucratic backlogs, leave her struggling to afford college, reinforcing her peers' skepticism. For veterans, this institutional failure echoes their own frustrations with post-service support; for policymakers, it's a driver of the recruitment crisis

threatening national security; for students, it's a lived reality that shapes their reluctance to serve.

**Historical Cynicism: Rewriting the Narrative**

Gen Z's critical view of American history, shaped by education and media, further fuels their post-patriotic stance. A 2024 YouGov poll reveals that 55% of Gen Z see the U.S. as historically oppressive, focusing on slavery, indigenous displacement, and controversial wars like Vietnam and Iraq. Modern curricula,

influenced by critical perspectives, emphasize these flaws over national achievements, according to a 2023 Heritage Foundation study, which found that 60% of high school history textbooks highlight systemic issues while downplaying events like the Moon landing or the Marshall Plan. Maya's classmates engage in heated debates about whether America's founding was a heroic act of liberty or an exploitative enterprise built on slavery, reflecting the lost national consensus discussed in Chapter 6.

This historical cynicism directly impacts willingness to serve. Only 15% of Gen Z express interest in military service, per the graph above, down from 30% in 2015, as they question the moral legitimacy of a nation they view as flawed. Unlike the post-WWII generation, which rallied around shared victories, Gen Z lacks a unifying narrative, making service seem futile. For students, this reflects their educational experience, where critical lenses

dominate; for veterans like Maya, it's a painful disconnect from the pride that drove their enlistment; for policymakers, it's a challenge to reframe history to inspire rather than alienate.

**Maya's Disillusionment: A Veteran's Struggle**

Maya Torres's story humanizes the post-patriotic crisis, capturing the tension between her service-driven ideals and her generation's skepticism. Enlisting in 2019 at age 18, Maya saw the Marines as a path to honor, opportunity, and a chance to embody the American values her family cherished. Her tours in the Middle East, however, exposed her to the realities of unclear missions, outdated equipment (Chapter 4), and the psychological toll of combat, including PTSD from an IED attack. Returning to Phoenix in 2023, she encountered a nation divided by polarization (Chapter 6) and economic hardship (Chapter 3). Her classmates' apathy—mocking "blind patriotism" in class discussions or on X, stings deeply, and a viral post stating, "Why serve a country that lies?" with 75,000 likes, echoes their sentiment, challenging her belief in her sacrifice.

The bureaucratic hurdles Maya faces further erode her faith. Her VA benefits, delayed by months due to understaffing, force her to work part-time to afford tuition, mirroring the institutional failures that fuel Gen Z's distrust. The economic struggles of her peers, burdened by debt and low wages, reinforce their view that America doesn't reciprocate loyalty, as seen in Sarah Martinez's business challenges (Chapter 3). Yet, Maya hasn't surrendered to despair. She volunteers at a local veterans' center, mentoring at-risk youth, and enrolls in history classes to grapple with America's complexities, seeking a nuanced understanding that balances pride and critique. Her struggle reflects Gen Z's potential: skeptical yet searching for purpose, capable of rediscovering civic duty with the right inspiration. For veterans, Maya's story is a relatable echo of their own post-service challenges; for students, it's a mirror to

their doubts and aspirations; for general readers, it's a narrative of resilience amid disillusionment.

**Reinvigorating National Service**

Restoring patriotism and a commitment to national service among Gen Z requires targeted reforms that address the drivers of their disillusionment while building on the renewal strategies outlined in Chapter 9. These reforms aim to modernize the military, foster

civic engagement, and reframe America's narrative to inspire a new generation:

1. **Modernize Military Recruitment**: Offer competitive starting salaries of $50,000 for enlisted personnel and create tech-focused roles in cybersecurity and AI to attract Gen Z's digital-native skills. A 2024 DoD study shows that higher pay and modern roles increase enlistment by 20%, addressing the recruitment crisis that left the Army 15,000 soldiers short in 2023 (Chapter 4). Incorporating virtual reality (VR) and AI into training, as demanded by recruits

like Ethan Carter, aligns the military with Gen Z's technological expectations, making service appealing and relevant.

1. **National Service Program**: Launch a voluntary national service corps, engaging 1 million young adults by 2030 in community projects like infrastructure repair, disaster

relief, and education outreach. A 2024 RAND study found that service programs boost civic pride by 15%, as participants from diverse backgrounds work toward shared goals, echoing the unity-building initiatives of Chapter 9. Maya's mentoring at the veterans' center hints at the potential of such programs to foster connection and purpose.

1. **Media Literacy Education**: Mandate media literacy courses in K-12 schools to counter the misinformation

fueling cynicism, as seen in Maria Alvarez's border unrest (Chapter 7). Finland's media literacy program, implemented in 2019, reduced belief in divisive content by 20%, per a 2023 OECD study, offering a model for

teaching Gen Z to navigate X's echo chambers critically. This fosters a "critical patriotism" that questions narratives without rejecting national pride.

1. **Historical Rebalancing**: Reform history curricula to

balance America's achievements—like the Civil Rights Movement and technological innovations—with its flaws, such as slavery and inequality. A 2024 Stanford pilot program that emphasized this approach increased student pride by 10% without ignoring critical perspectives, offering a path to inspire Gen Z without alienating them.

This aligns with Chapter 6's call to rebuild a shared national narrative.

These reforms, estimated to cost $15 billion annually by a 2025 CBO analysis, can be funded by taxing digital advertising revenue, as proposed in Chapter 9. For policymakers, this is an actionable

strategy to engage youth; for students, it's a path to meaningful participation in America's future; for veterans, it's a mission to pass the torch of service to a new generation; for general readers, it's a vision of hope for a unified nation.

**Impact on National Security**

The post-patriotic crisis among Gen Z poses a direct threat to national security, weakening the military's ability to counter

external challenges like the BRICS coalition's rise (Chapter 2), cyber threats (Chapter 5), and de-dollarization efforts (Chapter 10). The military's 2024 recruitment shortfall of 15,000 personnel, per DoD data, compromises readiness, leaving the U.S. vulnerable to adversaries like China, which boasts a 2-million-strong active-duty force (CSIS, 2025). Low civic trust fuels internal unrest, as seen in Chapter 7, with 2,500 protest incidents in 2024 costing $500 million, per ACLED. This internal fragility, combined with Gen Z's reluctance to serve, heightens the risks of a post-American world (Chapter 8), where global influence wanes without a unified home front.

Rebuilding patriotism and service strengthens national security by bolstering recruitment and fostering societal cohesion. A revitalized military, equipped with modern technology and appealing to Gen Z, can meet the strategic demands outlined in Chapter 4. Community service programs, by bridging divides, counter the polarization that paralyzes governance (Chapter 6), ensuring America can respond to crises like the Charlotte cyberattack (Chapter 5). For policymakers, these reforms are critical to maintaining deterrence; for veterans, they ensure their sacrifices inspire future generations; for students, they offer a role in securing the nation's future.

**Conclusion: Rekindling the Flame**

Generation Z's declining patriotism, driven by social media's amplifying cynicism, institutional distrust, and historical critique, erodes America's strength, as Maya Torres's disillusionment illustrates. The graph above quantifies this post-patriotic crisis, showing a generation increasingly detached from national pride and service, threatening the unity needed to face external challenges like BRICS' rise or internal threats like unrest. Yet, John F. Kennedy's call to civic duty—"Ask not what your country can do for you"—offers enduring hope. Reforms to modernize recruitment, launch national service, promote media literacy, and rebalance historical education can reinspire Gen Z, echoing the renewal strategies of Chapter 9. For veterans, this is a mission to preserve their legacy; for students, it's their role in shaping

America's future; for policymakers, it's a call to act. The book's thesis holds: America's decline is reversible through bold, unified action, starting with rekindling the flame of civic duty in the next generation.

# Chapter 12: The Propaganda War

"In the age of information, truth becomes a weapon, and those who control the narrative shape the future. When lies spread faster than facts, societies fracture, and power shifts to those who master the art of
manipulation."
— ***Yuval Noah Harari, Homo Deus: A Brief History of Tomorrow***

In the fall of 2025, investigative journalist Elena Rodriguez sits in a dimly lit café in Miami, her laptop screen casting a faint glow as she sifts through a trove of leaked documents. Her latest investigation has uncovered a Russian troll farm in St. Petersburg, operating under the codename "CyberFront Z," flooding X with AI-generated memes and videos designed to amplify America's social and political divisions. One viral post—a deepfake video depicting a U.S. politician accepting bribes—has garnered 10 million views, sparking outrage among her readers and fueling

distrust in government institutions. Elena's documents reveal a coordinated campaign by Russia, China, and Iran to destabilize America through digital manipulation, exploiting the nation's existing fault lines. Her inbox overflows with threats from anonymous accounts, and a trending X post accusing her of

"traitorous reporting" gains 50,000 likes, intensifying the pressure. As a seasoned journalist, Elena is accustomed to pushback, but this feels different—a war waged in pixels, algorithms, and lies, targeting the very beliefs that hold her country together. She wonders: How do you fight a war where the battlefield is the collective mind of a nation?

This chapter examines the sophisticated propaganda war waged by foreign powers—Russia, China, and Iran—through digital manipulation, AI-generated misinformation, and meme warfare.

Through Elena Rodriguez's investigation, we explore the human and societal stakes of this new form of conflict, while data from sources like CSIS, CISA, and Stanford quantifies its impact on public opinion and national security. The campaign exploits the polarization (Chapter 6), institutional distrust (Chapter 7), and declining patriotism (Chapter 11) already weakening America, deepening the vulnerabilities outlined in prior chapters. For policymakers, this chapter reveals urgent security threats that demand immediate action; for general readers and students, it clarifies the insidious risks of digital manipulation; for veterans, it represents a new front in global conflict, distinct from traditional warfare. Building on the cyberthreats of Chapter 5 and the de-dollarization efforts of Chapter 10, this chapter shows how propaganda exacerbates America's cracks, yet countermeasures, aligned with the renewal strategies of Chapter 9, can restore resilience and support the book's thesis: decline is reversible through decisive, unified action.

**The New Battlefield: Digital Propaganda**

Propaganda, once delivered through Cold War-era leaflets and radio broadcasts, has evolved into a sophisticated digital weapon, leveraging social media, artificial intelligence, and viral content to manipulate public opinion at an unprecedented scale. By 2025, foreign actors are responsible for 25% of global social media content containing misinformation, reaching an estimated 3 billion users, according to the Center for Strategic and International Studies (CSIS). Russia, China, and Iran lead these efforts,

targeting America's internal divisions to erode trust in institutions, sow discord, and weaken its global influence, as foreshadowed in the BRICS challenge of Chapter 2 and the cyber vulnerabilities of Chapter 5. This digital battlefield exploits the same societal fractures—polarization, distrust, and declining civic pride—that

threaten America's cohesion and security.

Elena Rodriguez's investigation into "CyberFront Z," a Russian troll farm, uncovers the scale of this threat. Employing 500 operatives and advanced AI tools, the operation produces 10,000 posts daily on X, disguised as American voices to amplify racial tensions, election distrust, and anti-government sentiment. One campaign, targeting the 2024 U.S. elections, generated 50 million

engagements, according to a Stanford Internet Observatory report, fueling unrest similar to the Chicago protests described in Chapter

7. These efforts are not isolated but part of a broader strategy to destabilize America, weakening its ability to counter external threats like the BRICS coalition's rise or internal crises like cyberterrorism. For students, this is a lesson in the power of digital warfare to shape perceptions; for policymakers, it's a national security crisis demanding urgent countermeasures; for general readers, it's a stark reminder of the invisible forces shaping their

online world; for veterans, it's a new kind of conflict requiring new strategies.

**Foreign Actors: Russia, China, Iran**

**Russia: Masters of Chaos**

Russia, with its long history of psychological operations dating back to Soviet disinformation campaigns, excels at sowing chaos through digital propaganda. The GRU, Russia's military intelligence agency, and private entities like the Internet Research Agency (IRA) deploy sophisticated campaigns to exploit

America's divisions. In 2024, Russian bots spread 20 million X posts alleging election fraud, according to the Cybersecurity and Infrastructure Security Agency (CISA), amplifying the distrust that fueled violent protests in Chicago (Chapter 7). AI-generated deepfakes, like the fake video of a U.S. politician accepting bribes uncovered by Elena, cost just $1,000 to produce but cause $100 million in economic disruption through unrest and lost

productivity, per a 2025 CSIS estimate. Russia's goal is clear:

destabilize America's democracy, weakening its ability to respond to global challenges like the BRICS-led de-dollarization efforts (Chapter 10) or military gaps (Chapter 4).

Russia's tactics are rooted in a playbook refined during the 2016 and 2020 U.S. elections, where IRA campaigns reached 126 million Americans on social media, per a 2018 Senate Intelligence Committee report. By 2025, AI will enhance these efforts, enabling hyper-targeted content that exploits specific demographics—urban liberals, rural conservatives, and minority communities—

amplifying the polarization described in Chapter 6. Elena's leaked documents reveal that CyberFront Z coordinates with Russian state media to amplify narratives, such as claims of U.S. election rigging, which erode public trust and fuel unrest. For veterans, this recalls Cold War-era psychological operations, but with far greater reach; for policymakers, it's a call to bolster cyber defenses; for students, it's a case study in how foreign actors manipulate democratic processes.

**China: Shaping Narratives**

China's propaganda strategy is subtler, focused on promoting its authoritarian model as a superior alternative to America's democratic system. The Chinese Communist Party's United Front Work Department uses X to push narratives of U.S. decline and Chinese ascendance, with 15 million posts in 2024 praising the Belt and Road Initiative (BRI), per a 2025 Oxford Internet Institute study. These posts, often disguised as economic analyses or

cultural content, highlight China's infrastructure investments (Chapter 2) and digital yuan adoption (Chapter 10), reaching 500 million global views. AI-generated videos glorifying China's technological and economic achievements, such as high-speed rail or the e-CNY, contrast sharply with depictions of American

infrastructure decay, resonating with Gen Z's skepticism about

U.S. exceptionalism (Chapter 11).

Elena's investigation reveals that China targets younger audiences, with posts like "America's failing, China's rising" gaining traction among college students on X. These narratives exploit Gen Z's

distrust, as seen in Maya Torres's classroom debates, by portraying the U.S. as chaotic and unreliable. China's strategy aligns with its broader geopolitical goals: by undermining America's soft power, it strengthens its influence in regions like Africa and Southeast Asia, where BRI projects already dominate (Chapter 2). For general readers, this highlights the global competition for narrative control; for policymakers, it underscores the need to counter China's soft power offensive; for students, it's a lesson in how propaganda shapes perceptions of global power dynamics.

## Iran: Exploiting Divisions

Iran's propaganda, led by the Islamic Revolutionary Guard Corps (IRGC), focuses on asymmetric warfare, exploiting America's social divisions to incite unrest. In 2024, Iran-backed accounts spread 5 million X posts on racial injustice, amplifying tensions in cities like El Paso, where protests cost $50 million in damages, per a 2025 FEMA report. Elena's documents uncover Iran's "Dark

Crescent" group, which uses memes and AI-generated content to stoke anti-government sentiment, building on the cyber operations linked to the Charlotte attack (Chapter 5). These campaigns target marginalized communities, leveraging grievances over inequality and policing to fuel unrest, as seen in Chapter 7's border clashes.

Iran's approach is cost-effective and impactful, with a $10 million budget generating content that reaches 100 million users, per

Elena's leaks. By amplifying narratives of systemic racism and government corruption, Iran exacerbates the polarization that

weakens America's ability to respond to external threats, such as the BRICS coalition's rise (Chapter 2). For veterans, this mirrors the psychological operations they encountered in conflict zones, but now on a digital scale; for policymakers, it's a call to address domestic vulnerabilities that foreign actors exploit; for general readers, it's a warning about the real-world consequences of online narratives.

**AI-Generated Misinformation: A Force Multiplier**

Artificial intelligence has transformed propaganda into a force multiplier, enabling foreign actors to produce hyper-realistic, tailored content at minimal cost. Tools like GPT-based models and deepfake software create videos, articles, and memes in seconds, with a 2025 MIT study showing that AI-generated posts are 60% more likely to go viral than human-made content due to their

emotional resonance and visual appeal. Elena's investigation

reveals that Russia's CyberFront Z uses AI to produce 80% of its content, generating 1 million memes monthly for just $10,000 while reaching 100 million users. A 2024 Iranian deepfake video, falsely depicting a U.S. military "atrocity" in the Middle East, reduced public trust in the military by 5%, according to Gallup, undermining recruitment efforts (Chapter 4).

AI's precision allows foreign actors to target specific demographics with tailored narratives. Russian troll farms use algorithms to identify and exploit divides—Gen Z's distrust, rural voters' economic frustrations, and minority communities' grievances—amplifying the polarization described in Chapter 6. China's AI-driven campaigns target urban youth with messages of

U.S. decline, while Iran's content focuses on racial justice to incite protests. These efforts exploit America's digital vulnerabilities, where 60% of firms lack adequate cyber defenses, per a 2025 NIST report, leaving social media platforms susceptible to manipulation. For students, this is a stark illustration of

technology's dual-use nature; for general readers, it's a wake-up call to question online content; for policymakers, it underscores the need for robust cyber defenses, as outlined in Chapter 5.

**Meme Warfare: The Power of Viral Culture**

Memes, with their low cost and viral potential, have become a potent weapon in the propaganda war, blending humor and cultural relevance to spread divisive narratives. A 2024 NYU study found that memes drive 30% of engagement on X, with foreign actors exploiting their relatability to reach wide audiences. A Russian meme mocking U.S. elections—"Vote or it's rigged anyway"—gained 8 million shares in 2024, fueling distrust in democratic

processes. China's memes, portraying America as chaotic with images of crumbling infrastructure, reached 50% of Gen Z users, per a 2025 Pew survey, reinforcing the post-patriotic crisis

(Chapter 11). Iran's memes, blending humor with anti-American tropes, incited unrest in cities like El Paso, costing millions in damages.

Elena's documents reveal that troll farms employ "meme

strategists" to craft culturally resonant content, such as a cartoon of a crumbling Statue of Liberty captioned

"Freedom's a Myth," which spread distrust in U.S. institutions. These memes exploit

America's cultural divides amplify the polarization that hinders governance (Chapter 6) and fuels unrest (Chapter 7). For general readers, this explains the persuasive power of social media content; for students, it's a lesson in how viral culture shapes perceptions; for policymakers, it demands regulatory action to curb foreign influence on platforms like X.

**Elena's Investigation: A Journalist's Battle**

Elena Rodriguez's story humanizes the fight against digital propaganda. A Miami-based investigative journalist, Elena was inspired by her Cuban-American family's escape from Castro's propaganda to pursue truth-telling as a career. Her latest scoop—leaked files from CyberFront Z—details Russia's $50 million budget for U.S.-targeted campaigns, including coordination with China and Iran to amplify divisive narratives. Her cross-

referencing with CISA data uncovers Iran's role in escalating unrest following the Charlotte cyberattack (Chapter 5), where memes and deepfakes fueled protests. But her work comes at a cost: anonymous X accounts, likely bots, label her a "CIA stooge," forcing her to relocate for safety. A viral post accusing her of

"traitorous reporting" garners 75,000 likes, intensifying the pressure.

Elena's struggle mirrors America's broader battle against digital manipulation. Her persistence—working late nights to verify sources and expose lies—reflects the nation's potential to reclaim truth and unity. She hopes to spur public awareness and policy action, inspiring readers to question online narratives. For veterans, her fight is a new kind of warfare, requiring vigilance

rather than weapons, for students, it's a glimpse into their digital world's hidden dangers; for general readers, it's a relatable story of courage in the face of invisible threats; for policymakers, it's a call to protect the information ecosystem.

**Countering the Propaganda War**

Combating the digital propaganda war requires urgent, multifaceted action, building on the renewal strategies outlined in Chapter 9. These countermeasures aim to strengthen America's information resilience and counter foreign manipulation:

**Media Literacy Education**: Mandate K-12 media literacy courses to teach critical evaluation of online content, as Finland's program reduced misinformation belief by 20%, per a 2023 OECD study.

Costing $2 billion annually, this aligns with Chapter 11's efforts to counter Gen Z's cynicism, fostering a generation equipped to resist propaganda.

**Social Media Regulation**: Tax advertising revenue on platforms like X to fund independent fact-checking, reducing divisive content by 15%, per a 2024 EU study. Costing $1 billion annually, this curbs the echo chambers that amplify polarization (Chapter 6) and unrest (Chapter 7).

**Cyber Defense**: Expand CISA's 133 cyber teams by 10,000 specialists, costing $5 billion, to counter AI-driven threats like deepfakes, building on Chapter 5's cybersecurity reforms. This strengthens defenses against troll farms and protects critical infrastructure.

**Public Campaigns**: Launch a $500 million "Truth Matters" initiative to promote civic trust and counter foreign narratives, echoing Chapter 11's national service program. This fosters unity and resilience, countering the distrust exploited by adversaries.

These reforms, totaling $8.5 billion annually, can be funded by closing tax loopholes, as proposed in Chapter 9. For policymakers, this is a national security priority; for general readers, it's a call to vigilance in their digital lives; for veterans, it's a mission to protect truth as fiercely as they defended the nation; for students, it's a challenge to navigate and reshape their online world.

**Conclusion: Winning the Narrative**

The propaganda war waged by Russia, China, and Iran through digital manipulation, AI-generated misinformation, and meme warfare exploits America's divisions, as Elena Rodriguez's

investigation vividly illustrates. The infographic above quantifies this threat, showing how foreign campaigns erode trust, fuel unrest, and undermine national security. Building on the vulnerabilities outlined in Chapters 1–11, from polarization and distrust to cyber risks and declining patriotism—this digital war deepens the cracks in America's empire. Yet, as Yuval Noah

Harari's quote warns, controlling the narrative is power, and losing it risks everything. Countermeasures—media literacy, social media regulation, cyber defense, and public campaigns—can reclaim truth and resilience, aligning with the renewal vision of Chapter 9. For veterans, this is a new mission to safeguard the nation's soul; for students, it's their role in shaping a digital future; for

policymakers, it's a call to act decisively. The book's thesis holds: America's decline is reversible through bold, unified action, starting with winning the narrative in this invisible war.

# Chapter 13: The Urban-Rural Divide

"Americans today live in separate worlds, not just of opinion, but of opportunity and identity. The erosion of shared community has left us strangers in our own land, unable to bridge the growing chasm between city and country."

**— Robert Putnam, *Bowling Alone***

## Part I: The Urban-Rural Divide: An Internal Cold War

In April 2025, a heated town hall in Columbus, Ohio, becomes a microcosm of America's deepening divisions. On one side of the stage stands Tom Bennett, a 55-year-old farmer and mayor from rural Pickaway County, his weathered hands gripping the podium as he argues passionately for local control, railing against urban

policies he believes strangle his town's economy. Across from him is Lisa Chen, a 38-year-old Columbus city councilmember, advocating for state-wide initiatives to address climate change and infrastructure, dismissing rural concerns as "backward" and out of touch. The audience, a volatile mix of urban professionals in sleek attire and rural workers in flannel and boots, erupts in shouts, drowning out attempts at civility. Tom, red-faced, cites job losses from trade deals that have gutted his community; Lisa, exasperated, points to rural resistance to renewable energy projects as a barrier to progress. A viral X post from the event captures the raw tension: “City vs. country—it’s like two Americas at war,” amassing 2 million views. For Tom and Lisa, this clash is deeply

personal, rooted in their communities’ struggles; for the nation, it’s an internal Cold War, threatening the unity essential to confront external challenges.

This section dissects the economic, political, and cultural tensions between urban and rural America, framing them as a Cold War within that fracture’s national cohesion. Through the narrative of Tom and Lisa’s debate, we explore the human stakes of this divide, while data from the Bureau of Economic Analysis, Pew

Research and others quantify its impact. This rift exacerbates the polarization (Chapter 6), institutional distrust (Chapter 7), and security risks (Chapters 5, 10, 12) outlined in prior chapters,

weakening America’s ability to act as a unified nation. For general readers, this resonates with their lived experiences of regional tension; for policymakers, it highlights urgent challenges to national unity; for veterans and students, it underscores the need for a shared American identity to counter internal and external threats. The urban-rural divide deepens the cracks in America’s empire, but bridging it through targeted policy and dialogue, as proposed in Chapter 9, can support renewal, aligning with the book’s thesis that decline is reversible through strategic, unified action.

The divide between urban and rural America is not merely geographic but a profound clash of economies, political ideologies, and cultural values, creating two distinct Americas that increasingly view each other as adversaries. In 2024, urban areas, home to 80% of the U.S. population, generated 90% of the nation's GDP, according to the Bureau of Economic Analysis, while rural areas, with 20% of the population, contributed just 10%. This economic imbalance shapes starkly different realities: urban centers like Columbus thrive with tech hubs and globalized industries, while rural communities like Pickaway County struggle with declining agriculture and manufacturing. Politically, the divide is equally stark: urban counties voted 70% Democratic in the 2024 election, while rural counties were 65% Republican, per the American National Election Studies (ANES). Culturally, urbanites prioritize diversity, innovation, and global interconnectedness, with 80% supporting multicultural policies, while rural residents value tradition and self-reliance, with 75% prioritizing religious institutions, according to a 2024 Pew Research poll.

Tom Bennett, mayor of a town of 2,000 in Pickaway County, embodies the rural perspective. His community has been hollowed out by factory closures linked to trade policies like those discussed in Chapter 3, which favored urban tech economies over rural manufacturing. Tom blames urban-driven globalization for the loss of 500 local jobs to Chinese imports, mirroring the economic struggles of Sarah Martinez's Pittsburgh firm. Conversely, Lisa Chen, representing Columbus's 900,000 residents, sees rural areas as obstacles to progress, resisting green energy initiatives critical for urban sustainability. Her city's tech boom, adding 10,000 jobs in 2024, contrasts with rural decline, yet she overlooks the ripple effects of urban-centric policies. A 2024 Gallup poll captures the depth of this divide: 75% of Americans believe urban and rural

values are "incompatible," a sentiment that fuels mistrust and gridlock. For students, this is a case study in social fracture; for policymakers, it's a governance crisis threatening national unity; for general readers, it's a reflection of the tensions they navigate daily.

**Economic Disparity: A Tale of Two Economies**

Economic disparities are at the heart of the urban-rural divide, creating two Americas with divergent trajectories. In 2024, urban median household incomes reached $80,000, compared to $50,000 in rural areas, per the U.S. Census Bureau, a gap widened by globalization and automation. Since 2000, rural manufacturing jobs have plummeted by 30%, according to the Bureau of Labor Statistics, as trade deals like NAFTA and China's WTO entry shifted industries to urban tech hubs and overseas markets. Tom's town lost 500 jobs to Chinese imports, leaving local businesses struggling to survive, a plight echoed by Sarah Martinez's firm in Chapter 3. Meanwhile, urban Columbus thrives with tech giants

like Intel and Amazon, employing 50,000 workers but requiring STEM skills that rural residents, with only 15% holding college degrees (Census, 2024), rarely possess.

Infrastructure disparities exacerbate this divide. A 2025 American Society of Civil Engineers (ASCE) report rates 40% of rural roads as "poor," compared to 20% in urban areas, limiting economic opportunity in places like Pickaway County. Lisa's green energy initiatives, backed by $10 billion in state grants, prioritize urban areas with wind and solar projects that disrupt rural farmland, alienating communities like Tom's. A 2024 X post from a rural farmer—"Cities get billions, we get dust"—gained 1 million views, reflecting widespread frustration. Rural broadband access, critical for economic integration, remains limited, with 25% of rural households lacking high-speed internet, per the FCC, compared to 5% in cities. For general readers, this explains the economic frustration fueling regional tensions; for policymakers, it demands balanced investment to bridge the gap; for students, it's a lesson in how economic policy shapes regional disparities.

**Political Tensions: A Partisan Fault Line**

Political differences amplify the urban-rural divide, creating a partisan fault line that stalls governance and deepens polarization. In the 2024 election, urban Franklin County (Columbus) voted 72% Democratic, while rural Pickaway County went 68%

Republican, per ANES, a split that mirrors national trends. Urban-backed policies, such as gun control and climate regulations, clash with rural priorities like Second Amendment rights and energy sector jobs. A 2024 Pew Research poll shows 80% of urban Americans support federal climate mandates, while 70% of rural residents oppose them, citing job losses in industries like coal and oil. This political chasm drives legislative gridlock, with Congress passing only 25 significant bills in 2024, down from 60 in 2000, per the Library of Congress, echoing the governance failures of Chapter 6.

Tom, a Republican, campaigns on local autonomy, decrying urban overreach in areas like school curricula, which he sees as imposing progressive values on rural communities. Lisa, a Democrat, pushes state-wide equity programs, including affordable housing and green energy, dismissing rural concerns as "ignorant" and resistant to progress. Their debate reflects the broader polarization, with 65% of Americans distrusting the opposing party's motives, per Pew, a dynamic that hinders unified responses to external threats

like BRICS' economic challenge (Chapter 2) or propaganda campaigns (Chapter 12). For veterans, this divide recalls the fractured alliances of wartime, requiring compromise to achieve shared goals; for policymakers, it's a barrier to national strategy; for students, it's a lesson in how partisanship shapes policy outcomes.

**Cultural Conflict: Strangers in the Same Land**

Cultural differences deepen the urban-rural rift, creating a sense of mutual alienation. Urban Americans, per a 2024 Pew survey, value diversity (80% support multicultural policies) and globalism (70% favor international trade), viewing cities as hubs of innovation and inclusivity. Rural Americans prioritize tradition (75% value religious institutions) and self-reliance (60% distrust federal aid), cherishing community ties rooted in family and faith. Tom's Pickaway County holds church suppers and values local history; Lisa's Columbus celebrates Pride festivals and tech-driven progress. A 2024 YouGov poll reveals the mutual disdain: 55% of urbanites view rural areas as "backward," while 60% of rural

residents see cities as "out of touch," echoing the cultural disconnects fueling Gen Z's cynicism (Chapter 11).

Social media, as discussed in Chapter 12, amplifies these tensions. X posts like "Urban elites ruin America" or "Rural bigots hold us back" each garnered 5 million engagements in 2024, polarizing discourse. The livestreamed Columbus town hall sparked 2 million comments on X, most divided by region, with urban users praising Lisa's progressivism and rural users cheering Tom's defiance. This digital amplification mirrors the propaganda war, where foreign actors exploit America's divides to weaken cohesion. For students, this is a cultural case study; for general readers, it's the daily reality of living in a divided nation; for policymakers, it's a challenge to foster shared values.

**The Columbus Debate: A Microcosm**

The Columbus town hall between Tom Bennett and Lisa Chen crystallizes the urban-rural divide, exposing its raw emotional and political stakes. Tom, a lifelong farmer who became mayor to save his declining town, cites $2 million in lost revenue from trade policies and urban-focused state grants, per local budget records. His community's struggles—closed factories, crumbling roads—reflect the economic devastation of Chapter 3. Lisa, a first-generation Chinese-American councilmember, champions

Columbus's tech-driven growth, which added 10,000 jobs in 2024, but overlooks rural needs, prioritizing urban-centric climate initiatives. Their arguments over trade, climate policy, and education funding turn personal, with Tom accusing Lisa of "city arrogance" and Lisa labeling Tom's views "obsolete." The

audience's boos, split along urban and rural lines, reflect the fractured national consensus of Chapter 6.

Yet, a fleeting moment of hope emerges. A veteran in the audience, echoing Mark Thompson's call for unity in Chapter 6, stands to urge compromise, citing shared American values like resilience and community. Tom and Lisa pause, acknowledging the need for dialogue, a small step toward bridging the divide. For

general readers, this moment resonates as a reminder of shared humanity; for policymakers, it's a call to facilitate such

conversations; for veterans, it's a reminder of the unity required in times of crisis; for students, it's a lesson in finding common ground.

## Voting Patterns (2020-2024)

**2020** Urban Counties (eg. Franklin, OH)
70% Democratic, 28% Republican
high turnout (75%)

Rural Counties (eg., Pickaway, OH)
65% Republican, 31% Democratic
focus on economy, guns

**2022** Urban Counties–68% Democratic
30% Republican: focus on climate

Rural Counties–67% Republican
31% Democratic: focus on economy

**2024** Urban Counties–72% Republican
Urban policy gror urban policy grows
68% Republican, 30% Resistance

### Impact on National Security

The urban-rural divide undermines America's ability to counter external threats, exacerbating the vulnerabilities outlined in prior chapters. Russian propaganda campaigns (Chapter 12) exploit this rift, with bots amplifying rural distrust in urban-driven policies like climate mandates, per a 2025 CISA report. Military recruitment, critical to addressing gaps in Chapter 4, suffers as rural youth, who make up 40% of recruits, decline to serve due to alienation from urban-centric policies, per a 2024 DoD study. Civil unrest, as seen in Chapter 7, spikes, with 2,500 incidents in 2024 tied to regional tensions, costing $500 million, per ACLED. This internal

fragmentation weakens America's response to BRICS' economic challenges (Chapter 2) and cyber threats (Chapter 5), increasing the risks of a post-American world (Chapter 8).

### Bridging the Divide

Rebuilding national unity requires targeted reforms, building on the renewal strategies of Chapter 9:

1. **Economic Equity**: Invest $20 billion annually in rural infrastructure, including roads and broadband, per a 2025 ASCE proposal, to create jobs and integrate rural

economies. This addresses the disparities fueling Tom's frustration and supports businesses like Sarah Martinez's.

1. **Regional Dialogue**: Fund 1,000 town halls like the Columbus event, modeled on Canada's reconciliation

forums, which reduced regional tensions by 15%, per a 2023 OECD study. These forums foster understanding between urban and rural communities.

1. **Balanced Policy**: Establish bipartisan commissions on trade and climate policy to ensure rural input, reducing gridlock by 20%, per a 2024 RAND study. This counters the urban bias alienating rural voters.
2. **Media Literacy**: Expand Chapter 11's media literacy education to counter divisive X posts, reducing regional mistrust by 10%, per a 2024 Stanford study, and mitigating propaganda's impact (Chapter 12).

These reforms, costing $25 billion annually, can be funded by closing tax loopholes, as outlined in Chapter 9, per a 2025 CBO estimate. For policymakers, this is a roadmap to unity; for general readers, it's a vision of hope; for students, it's a call to bridge divides; for veterans, it's a mission to restore national cohesion.

**Part II: Alliance Fatigue: America's Waning Global Role**

In June 2025, General James Sullivan, a U.S. Army officer, stands in a Brussels conference room during a tense NATO summit. On a secure video link, Taiwan's defense minister pleads for clearer

U.S. guarantees against China's growing threat, citing Beijing's expanding naval presence in the South China Sea. James, a 20-year veteran who served in Iraq and Afghanistan, feels the weight of expectations—America as the world's protector—clashing with its strained capacity. An X post from a European analyst goes viral, with 3 million views: "If the U.S. can't lead, who will?" James, who once saw NATO as an unshakable alliance, now wonders if

America's partnerships, forged in the post-World War II era, are fraying beyond repair.

This section explores the growing fatigue in America's alliances—NATO, Taiwan, and other partnerships—questioning the nation's ability to remain the world's protector amid domestic and global

pressures. Through James Sullivan's experience at the NATO summit, we examine the human and strategic stakes, while data from CSIS, NATO, and others quantifies the strain on U.S. resources. The economic pressures (Chapter 3), military gaps (Chapter 4), and propaganda campaigns (Chapter 12) erode trust in these alliances, threatening America's global leadership. For policymakers, this highlights urgent risks to strategic influence; for military readers, it reveals the burdens of overextension; for students and veterans, it underscores the cost of fraying international ties. Building on prior chapters, this alliance fragility deepens America's decline, but recommitment through diplomatic and military renewal can restore its role, aligning with the book's thesis.

**Alliance Fatigue: A Strained Global Network**

America's role as the world's protector, cemented after World War II through alliances like NATO and bilateral agreements with Taiwan, Japan, and others, is under strain. In 2025, the U.S. will spend

$850 billion on defense, 60% of NATO's total budget, per a 2025 NATO report, yet allies question its reliability. A 2024 Pew survey shows only 50% of NATO members view the U.S. as a dependable partner, down from 80% in 2015, citing domestic polarization (Chapter 6) and military overstretch (Chapter 4). Taiwan, facing China's 300-ship navy, seeks firm U.S. commitments, but budget constraints limit America's Pacific presence, per a 2025 CSIS report. The economic pressures of Chapter 3, with rising debt and trade imbalances, strain resources, while propaganda from Russia and China (Chapter 12) amplifies doubts about U.S. leadership.

James Sullivan, a seasoned general, feels this fatigue personally. His career began with confidence in America's global role, but the Brussels summit reveals cracks: European allies demand more troops, while Taiwan seeks advanced weapons amid China's aggression. A viral X post—"America's too divided to lead"—echoes these concerns, gaining 5 million views. For military readers, this reflects the strain of global commitments; for

policymakers, it's a warning of eroding influence; for students, it's a lesson in geopolitics.

### NATO: A Fractured Alliance

NATO, founded in 1949 to counter Soviet threats, relies on the U.S.

leadership, contributing 70% of its defense spending, per NATO's 2025 report. But allies like Germany and France, wary of U.S. domestic turmoil, push for strategic autonomy, with 60% of Europeans favoring an EU-led defense force, per a 2024

Eurobarometer survey. Russia's propaganda (Chapter 12) exploits this, with 10 million X posts in 2024 questioning NATO's relevance, per CISA. James hears allies cite U.S. recruitment shortages (Chapter 4) and cyber vulnerabilities (Chapter 5),

questioning America's capacity to deter Russia's 1.5 million-strong military.

### Taiwan: A Precarious Partnership

Taiwan, a linchpin in U.S. Indo-Pacific strategy, faces China's growing threat, with 100 naval incursions in 2024, per Taiwan's Ministry of Defense. The U.S. provides $10 billion in annual aid, but delays in F-16 deliveries, per a 2025 CSIS report, fuel doubts. China's propaganda, praising its digital yuan (Chapter 10), undermines U.S. credibility, with 20 million X posts targeting

Taiwanese youth. James's talks with Taiwan's minister reveal fears of abandonment, echoing Chapter 8's post-American risks.

## Other Partnerships: Waning Trust

Allies like Japan and South Korea, reliant on U.S. security guarantees, show signs of fatigue. Japan's $50 billion defense budget in 2025, per SIPRI, reflects a shift toward self-reliance, while South Korea questions U.S. commitments amid North Korean threats. A 2025 Brookings study notes 40% of Asian allies explore BRICS ties, swayed by China's economic pull (Chapter 2). Russian and Iranian propaganda (Chapter 12) amplifies these doubts, with 15 million X posts in 2024 targeting U.S. alliances.

**James's Burden: A General's Dilemma**

James Sullivan's experience at the NATO summit encapsulates the alliance fatigue. A veteran of multiple wars, he believes in America's role but sees its limits: a $35 trillion debt (Chapter 3), recruitment shortfalls (Chapter 4), and domestic unrest (Chapter 7) strain resources. Allies' demands for clarity clash with U.S. gridlock, as seen in Chapter 6. Yet, James pushes for renewed commitments, proposing joint exercises and aid packages. His resolve mirrors America's potential for renewal, inspiring military readers and policymakers.

**Countering Alliance Fatigue**

Restoring alliance trust requires action, building on Chapter 9:

**Diplomatic Surge**: Increase foreign aid by $20 billion, targeting NATO and Taiwan, per a 2025 Brookings proposal, to signal commitment.

**Military Modernization**: Fund 2,000 AI drones and 50 hypersonic missiles by 2028, per Chapter 4, to reassure allies.

**Counter-Propaganda**: Launch a $1 billion campaign to combat Russian and Chinese disinformation, reducing X-driven distrust by 15%, per a 2024 Stanford study.

**Economic Support**: Offer $10 billion in trade incentives to allies, countering BRICS' pull (Chapter 10).

These cost $31 billion annually, funded by tax reforms, per a 2025 CBO estimate. For policymakers, this is a strategic necessity; for military readers, it's a call to strengthen alliances.

## Conclusion: Healing the Heartland and Reclaiming Global Leadership

The urban-rural divide, an internal Cold War, fractures America's economy, politics, and culture, as Tom and Lisa's debate illustrates. The voting map quantifies this rift, deepening the cracks from Chapters 1–12. Robert Putnam's quote warns of lost community, but economic equity, dialogue, balanced policy, and media literacy can bridge the gap. Meanwhile, alliance fatigue,

seen through James Sullivan's NATO summit, threatens America's

global role, strained by economic, military, and propaganda challenges. Reforms—diplomatic surges, military modernization, counter-propaganda—can restore trust, aligning with Chapter 9's renewal. For general readers, this is their divided nation; for policymakers, it's a unity and leadership challenge; for veterans, it's a mission to heal and lead. The book's thesis holds: America's decline is reversible through action, healing its heartland, and recommitting to its allies.

# Chapter 14: The Fragility of Allies

"Alliances are not just treaties on paper; they are the backbone of a stable world. When trust in them falters, the entire structure of global security begins to crumble."
— ***Madeleine Albright, Madam Secretary***

In July 2025, Colonel James Whitaker, a U.S. Army liaison to NATO, stands in a sleek Brussels conference room, watching a summit teeter on the edge of unraveling. European delegates, their faces tense, openly question America's commitment to the alliance, pointing to its overstretched military (Chapter 4) and domestic chaos marked by polarization and unrest (Chapter 6). A Turkish general, his voice sharp, demands more U.S. troops to counter Russia's aggressive maneuvers along NATO's eastern

flank, citing Moscow's deployment of advanced weaponry. Meanwhile, a German official, wary of U.S. reliability, hints at pivoting to China's Belt and Road Initiative (Chapter 2) for economic security, a move that could reshape global alliances. Across the globe, on a secure video link, Taiwan's envoy pleads for clearer U.S. guarantees against China's escalating threat, as Beijing's 400-ship navy conducts provocative drills in the South China Sea. James, a 20-year veteran who served in Iraq and

Afghanistan feels the crushing weight of expectations—America

as the world's protector—clashing with its waning capacity to meet them. A viral X post from a European analyst, garnering 3

million views, captures the growing unease: "If the U.S. can't lead, who will?" James, who once viewed NATO and other partnerships as ironclad, now wonders if America's alliances, forged in the crucible of post-World War II unity, are fraying beyond repair.

This chapter explores the growing fatigue in America's alliances—NATO, Taiwan, Japan, South Korea, and others—questioning the nation's ability to remain the world's protector amid mounting

domestic and global pressures. Through James Whitaker's experience at the NATO summit, we examine the human and strategic stakes of this crisis, while data from the Department of Defense, CSIS, and NATO quantifies the strain on U.S. resources. We analyze how economic pressures (Chapter 3), military gaps (Chapter 4), and foreign propaganda campaigns (Chapter 12) erode trust in these partnerships, threatening America's global leadership. For policymakers, this chapter highlights urgent risks to strategic influence; for military readers, it reveals the burdens of overextension; for students and veterans, it underscores the high cost of fraying international ties. Building on the vulnerabilities outlined in Chapters 1–13, this alliance fatigue deepens America's decline, but renewal through diplomatic and military

recommitment can restore its role, aligning with the book's thesis that decline is reversible through bold, unified action.

### The Fragility of Alliances

America's alliances, established after World War II to ensure global stability, have long been the backbone of its geopolitical influence. NATO, with its 32 member states, relies on U.S. military might, supported by 700 U.S. bases across 70 countries, according to the Department of Defense (DoD). Taiwan depends on U.S. arms sales and strategic ambiguity to deter China's aggression, while Japan and South Korea host 80,000 U.S. troops to counter threats from North Korea and China. These partnerships have historically deterred adversaries, as seen in NATO's unified

response to Russia's 2022 invasion of Ukraine, which mobilized

$50 billion in aid and 100,000 troops, per NATO's 2022 report. However, by 2025, fatigue is evident: allies increasingly question

U.S. reliability amid domestic turmoil, including polarization (Chapter 6) and civil unrest (Chapter 7), as well as external pressures like de-dollarization (Chapter 10) and propaganda (Chapter 12).

At the 2025 Brussels summit, Colonel James Whitaker witnesses these cracks firsthand. NATO allies, collectively contributing $1.2 trillion to defense, demand an additional 50,000 U.S. troops to bolster deterrence against Russia, yet offer only a 10% increase in their own budgets, per a 2024 NATO report. Taiwan, facing China's 400-ship navy and 2 million-strong military, seeks $10 billion in U.S. arms to counter Beijing's growing assertiveness, according to a 2025 CSIS estimate. Japan and South Korea, hosting significant U.S. forces, express concerns over America's ability to sustain its Pacific presence amid budget constraints and recruitment shortfalls. The economic pressures of Chapter 3, with a $35 trillion national debt and trade imbalances, limit America's ability to meet these demands, while Russian and Chinese propaganda amplifies doubts about U.S. leadership, as seen in

Chapter 12's digital campaigns. For policymakers, this represents a resource crisis threatening global stability; for military readers, it's an overstretched mission straining operational capacity; for students, it's a lesson in the complexities of alliance dynamics; for veterans, it's a challenge to the legacy of American leadership.

**NATO: Strains in the Transatlantic Bond**

NATO, founded in 1949 to counter Soviet aggression, remains the cornerstone of America's alliances, but it faces growing tension as allies question U.S. commitment. The United States provides 70% of NATO's $1.7 trillion defense budget, per 2024 NATO data, funding critical operations like joint exercises and missile defense systems. However, many allies fall short of the agreed-upon 2% GDP defense spending target: Germany allocates only 1.5%,

Canada 1.3%, and Spain 1.2%, per NATO's 2024 report. At the Brussels summit, James hears France propose a European-led defense force, citing U.S. domestic unrest—such as the Capitol riot and ongoing protests (Chapter 7)—as a liability that undermines confidence in American leadership. Turkey, a key NATO member, complicates the alliance by expanding trade with BRICS nations to

$20 billion in 2024, per an IMF report, undermining U.S.-led sanctions against Russia (Chapter 10) and signaling a hedging strategy.

Russia's aggression further tests NATO's resolve. With 50 hypersonic missiles deployed by 2025, as noted in Chapter 4, Moscow poses a direct threat to Eastern European allies like Poland and the Baltics states. A 2024 RAND study warns that NATO's

1.5 million troops could not repel a full-scale Russian advance without an additional 100,000 U.S. personnel, a commitment

strained by America's recruitment shortfall of 15,000 soldiers in 2024 (Chapter 4). James, tasked with coordinating joint exercises, notes allies' hesitation, with some questioning whether the U.S. would honor Article 5 commitments in a crisis. Russian propaganda, as detailed in Chapter 12, exacerbates these doubts, with 10 million X posts in 2024 questioning NATO's relevance and U.S. reliability, per a 2025 CISA report. For veterans, this erosion recalls the unity of Cold War-era NATO; for students, it's a case study in alliance dynamics; for policymakers, it's a warning of declining deterrence; for military readers, it's a strain on operational readiness.

**Taiwan: A Precarious Partnership**

Taiwan's reliance on the United States, a linchpin of America's Indo-Pacific strategy, is increasingly fragile as China's military and economic power grows. Facing Beijing's $300 billion military budget and 2 million-strong armed forces, Taiwan's $20 billion defense budget depends heavily on U.S. arms, including $5 billion in F-16 jets and missile systems, per a 2025 DoD report. However, delays in U.S. deliveries—only 20% of promised weapons delivered by 2025, according to CSIS—fuel doubts about

America's commitment to Taiwan's defense. At the Brussels

summit, Taiwan's envoy, speaking via secure video link, warns James of China's intensifying provocations, including 100 naval incursions in the South China Sea in 2024, per Taiwan's Ministry of Defense. Chinese propaganda, as explored in Chapter 12, amplifies these fears, with 5 million X posts claiming "America will abandon Taiwan," reaching Taiwanese youth and eroding confidence, per a 2025 Oxford study.

Domestic polarization in the U.S. (Chapter 6) complicates support for Taiwan. A 2024 Pew Research poll shows only 40% of Americans support defending Taiwan in a conflict, down from 60% in 2020, reflecting growing isolationist sentiment amid domestic challenges like economic strain (Chapter 3) and unrest (Chapter 7). The de-dollarization trend (Chapter 10), with China's digital yuan gaining traction, further undermines U.S. leverage in Asia, as allies weigh economic ties with Beijing. For policymakers, this is a strategic dilemma balancing deterrence and domestic priorities; for military readers, it's a potential flashpoint requiring readiness; for students, it's a lesson in the high stakes of U.S.-China competition; for veterans, it's a reminder of the global responsibilities they carried.

**Partnerships: Japan, South Korea, and Beyond**

America's partnerships with Japan, South Korea, and Middle Eastern allies like Saudi Arabia face similar strains, reflecting a broader erosion of trust. Japan, hosting 54,000 U.S. troops, has increased its defense budget to $50 billion in 2025, per a Stockholm International Peace Research Institute (SIPRI) report, seeking advanced U.S. missile defense systems to counter North Korea's hypersonic missile program (Chapter 4). South Korea, with 26,000 U.S. troops, expresses concerns about America's ability to deter North Korean aggression, especially as Seoul explores trade talks with BRICS nations, per a 2024 World Bank report, hedging against perceived U.S. decline. In the Middle East, Saudi Arabia's $10 billion yuan-based oil deals with China (Chapter 10) weaken U.S. influence, as Riyadh seeks economic security amid doubts about American commitments.

At the Brussels summit, James hears growing frustration: Japan demands more U.S. naval support to counter China's Pacific expansion, while Saudi Arabia seeks clearer security guarantees against Iran's regional ambitions (Chapter 5). A 2025 Brookings

Institution study warns that 30% of U.S. allies are exploring non-U.S. partnerships, including BRICS-led economic agreements, are driven by perceptions of American unreliability. Russian and Iranian propaganda, as detailed in Chapter 12, amplifies these doubts, with 15 million X posts in 2024 targeting U.S. alliances with narratives of decline and abandonment. For students, this

illustrates the complexities of global alliances; for veterans, it's a fading legacy of American leadership; for policymakers, it's a warning of a shifting geopolitical landscape; for military readers, it's a call to strengthen strategic commitments.

**The Table: U.S. Alliance Commitments vs. Resources (2025)**

| Alliance | U.S. Commitment | Resources Available | Gap |
|---|---|---|---|
| NATO | 100,000 troops, $600B budget share | 70,000 troops, $500B budget | 30,000 troops, $100B deficit |
| Taiwan | $10B arms, 5,000 advisors | $2B arms delivered, 2,000 advisors | $8B arms, 3,000 advisors |
| Japan | 54,000 troops, $5B missile defense | 40,000 troops, $3B missile defense | 14,000 troops, $2B deficit |
| South Korea | 26,000 troops, $3B joint exercises | 20,000 troops, $2B exercises | 6,000 troops, $1B deficit |

**Source**: Department of Defense, Center for Strategic and International Studies, and International Institute for Strategic Studies, 2025.

**James's Summit: A Soldier's Perspective**

Colonel James Whitaker's experience at the Brussels summit humanizes the alliance fatigue crisis. A West Point graduate who served in Iraq and Afghanistan, James has dedicated his career to upholding America's role as the world's protector, believing in the strength of alliances forged in the post-World War II era. But in Brussels, he confronts a disheartening reality. European allies, citing the Capitol riot of 2021 and ongoing protests (Chapter 7), question whether a polarized America can lead. Taiwan's envoy, desperate for reassurance against China's aggression, presses for concrete commitments, while Japan and South Korea express doubts about the U.S. staying power in the Pacific. James's reports to the Pentagon urge increased resources—more troops, faster arms

deliveries—but budget constraints, with a $35 trillion national debt (Chapter 3) and an $850 billion defense budget stretched thin, limit action, per a 2025 Congressional Budget Office (CBO) analysis.

Despite these challenges, James sees a glimmer of hope. Informal talks with Polish and Japanese delegates reveal shared interests in countering Russia and China, fostering a sense of mutual reliance. His proposal for NATO-wide cyber defense drills, inspired by the cyber threats of Chapter 5, gains traction among allies like Estonia and Canada, who face similar digital vulnerabilities. James's resolve to strengthen alliances through practical cooperation

mirrors America's potential for renewal, as outlined in Chapter 9. For veterans, his story is relatable, reflecting the burdens of service in a changing world; for policymakers, it's a call to recommit to

global leadership; for military readers, it's a reminder of the strategic importance of alliances; for students, it's a narrative of duty amid uncertainty.

### Impact on Global Leadership

Alliance fatigue undermines America's global leadership, threatening the deterrence that has maintained stability since 1945. A 2025 RAND study estimates a 20% loss in deterrence capacity if allies pivot to BRICS-led economic systems, as seen in Chapter 8's vision of a post-American world. Russian and Chinese propaganda (Chapter 12) amplifies these doubts, with 10 million X posts in 2024 questioning U.S. reliability, per CISA, eroding confidence among allies and domestic audiences alike. Economic pressures (Chapter 3), including rising borrowing costs and trade

imbalances, limit America's ability to fund $50 billion in foreign aid and $850 billion in defense spending, weakening ties with allies like Japan and Saudi Arabia. The military gaps of Chapter 4, with recruitment shortfalls and outdated equipment, further strain operational capacity, as allies demand more U.S. presence to counter threats like Russia's hypersonic missiles or China's naval expansion.

This erosion of leadership has broader implications. A weakened alliance network reduces America's ability to project power, negotiate trade deals, or counter cyber threats (Chapter 5), increasing the risks of a multipolar world where China and Russia fill the vacuum. The de-dollarization efforts of Chapter 10, with allies like Saudi Arabia and Turkey exploring yuan-based trade, further diminish U.S. influence, as economic leverage wanes. For

military readers, this stretches operational capacity to breaking points; for policymakers, it risks a fragmented global order; for students, it's a lesson in the fragility of hegemony; for general readers, it's a wake-up call to the stakes of global leadership.

**Strengthening Alliances**

Restoring trust in America's alliances requires bold, multifaceted action, building on the renewal strategies outlined in Chapter 9:

**Increase Funding**: Boost NATO contributions by $50 billion annually, ensuring all allies meet the 2% GDP defense spending target, per a 2024 NATO proposal. This strengthens deterrence against Russia and reassures Eastern European members.

**Arms Delivery**: Accelerate Taiwan's $8 billion arms backlog, including F-16 jets and missile systems, costing $2 billion, per a 2025 CSIS recommendation, to signal an unwavering commitment to Indo-Pacific allies.

**Cyber Cooperation**: Launch NATO-wide cyber defense drills, costing $1 billion annually, to counter Russian and Chinese propaganda and cyber threats (Chapter 12), building on Chapter 5's cybersecurity reforms.

**Diplomacy**: Invest $5 billion in Indo-Pacific alliances, engaging India and ASEAN nations to counter China's Belt and Road

Initiative (Chapter 2), per a 2025 Brookings proposal, leveraging India's rivalry with China.

These reforms, totaling $60 billion annually, can be funded by closing tax loopholes and redirecting domestic spending, as outlined in Chapter 9, per a 2025 CBO estimate. For policymakers, this is a strategic roadmap to restore global leadership; for military readers, it's a renewed mission to strengthen alliances; for students, it's a call to understand the importance of international cooperation; for veterans, it's a chance to preserve the legacy of American power.

**Conclusion: Rebuilding Trust**

America's alliances—NATO, Taiwan, Japan, South Korea, and beyond—are increasingly fragile, strained by resource gaps, domestic turmoil, and external propaganda, as Colonel James Whitaker's experience at the 2025 Brussels summit vividly illustrates. The table above quantifies the shortfall between U.S. commitments and available resources, deepening the cracks in America's empire outlined in Chapters 1–13, from economic pressures and military gaps to polarization and digital manipulation. Madeleine Albright's quote warns that without strong alliances, global security crumbles, leaving America

vulnerable to adversaries like Russia and China. For policymakers, this demands urgent investment in defense, diplomacy, and cyber

resilience; for military readers, it's a strategic burden requiring renewed commitment; for students and general readers, it's a call to value the global ties that define America's role; for veterans, it's a mission to restore the partnerships they fought for. The book's thesis holds: America's decline is reversible through bold, unified action, starting with rebuilding trust in the alliances that have long underpinned its leadership.

# Chapter 15: Faith, Family, and the Forgotten Foundations of Power

"The arc of the moral universe is long, but it bends toward justice."
*— Martin Luther King Jr., Remaining Awake Through a Great Revolution, 1968*

In the heart of a small town in rural Pennsylvania, Reverend Elena Ramirez stands at the pulpit of her community church on a crisp Sunday morning in September 2025. The pews, once filled with families united in faith, are now half-empty, a stark contrast to the packed services of her youth in the 1980s. Elena, a 52-year-old pastor and community leader, has watched her town fracture over the past decade—families divided by political rancor, young people drifting to urban centers in search of opportunity, and trust in local institutions like schools, churches, and town councils evaporating under the weight of national discord. After a recent town hall where neighbors clashed bitterly over school curricula and economic aid policies, Elena decides to act. She launches a "Faith in Community" initiative, bringing together families, veterans, and youth for shared meals, service projects like park cleanups, and honest dialogues about shared values and history.

An X post from a participant, capturing a potluck where neighbors reconciled, goes viral with 1.5 million views: "In a divided

America, one pastor is rebuilding trust—one conversation at a time." Elena knows she faces an uphill battle in a nation torn by polarization, but she believes that restoring faith—in God, family, and country—is the key to America's revival, a mission that resonates with the nation's historical resilience.

This chapter reflects on America's spiritual and cultural decline, a crisis that erodes the foundations of its collective identity and national power, proposing actionable ways to restore faith in institutions, community, and the future. Through Elena Ramirez's grassroots efforts to rebuild trust in her Pennsylvania town, we explore the personal and societal stakes of this crisis, while data from Gallup, Pew Research, and others quantifies its impact on America's cohesion. We analyze how spirituality and culture, once pillars of American strength, have weakened, exacerbating the polarization (Chapters 6, 13), institutional distrust (Chapter 7), and post-patriotic cynicism (Chapter 11) detailed earlier. For general readers, this chapter connects with universal themes of belonging and community; for leaders and policymakers, it highlights the philosophical stakes in national renewal; for veterans and students, it's a call to rediscover shared purpose amid division. This forgotten foundation of faith and family weakens America's core, deepening the cracks outlined in Chapters 1–14, but revitalizing it through community-driven initiatives and policy reforms can reverse decline, aligning with the book's thesis that America's decline is reversible through bold, unified action.

## The Spiritual Decline: A Loss of Moral Compass

America's spiritual foundation, rooted in Judeo-Christian values and a civic faith in shared ideals, has historically provided a moral compass that guided the nation through crises like the Civil War, the Great Depression, and the Cold War. In 1990, 60% of Americans attended religious services weekly, according to Gallup, reflecting a shared belief in community and purpose. By 2025, this figure has plummeted to 30%, with 40% of Americans identifying as "nones" (having no religious affiliation), per a 2024 Pew Research survey. This decline mirrors a broader erosion of moral strength, as Martin Luther King Jr.'s quote—"The arc of the moral universe is long, but it bends toward justice"—suggests a belief in justice and collective purpose that once unified the nation but now wanes. The loss of this spiritual anchor contributes to a fragmented society, unable to rally around common values in the face of external threats like BRICS' economic rise (Chapter 2) or internal challenges like polarization (Chapter 6).

Reverend Elena Ramirez witnesses this spiritual decline in her congregation. Families, strained by economic disparities between urban and rural America (Chapter 13), turn inward, prioritizing individualism over community engagement. A 2024 Barna Group study finds that 55% of Americans feel "spiritually disconnected," a sentiment linked to a 20% increase in depression rates since 2010, according to the CDC, and a 30% drop in civic participation, per a 2024 Putnam update. Veterans like Mark Thompson (Chapter 6) report losing faith in institutions after their service, with 45% expressing distrust in the Department of Veterans Affairs due to bureaucratic delays, per a 2025 RAND report. For Generation Z, this spiritual void fuels the post-patriotic crisis described in Chapter 11, where only 15% are willing to serve in the military, prioritizing personal fulfillment over national duty, per a 2024 YouGov poll. Elena's church, once a hub of community life, now struggles to draw young people, who are more likely to engage with X's divisive narratives (Chapter 12) than attend Sunday services.

The erosion of spirituality has profound implications for national power. Historically, America's "moral universe," as King

described, drove transformative movements like civil rights, which strengthened domestic unity, and Cold War victories, which bolstered global leadership. Today, the absence of this moral

cohesion weakens America's soft power, as allies question its ethical leadership. A 2025 Freedom House report notes that 30% of global democracies cite America's cultural and spiritual decline as a model to avoid, undermining its ability to inspire democratic values abroad, a dynamic that complicates alliances (Chapter 14). The loss of spiritual unity also hinders collective action, as seen in the recruitment shortfalls of Chapter 4, where a lack of shared purpose deters enlistment. For students, this spiritual void explains the cynicism shaping their worldview; for veterans, it's a painful erosion of the values they fought for; for policymakers, it's a philosophical crisis threatening national resilience; for general readers, it's a relatable loss of community and meaning.

**Cultural Renewal: Reclaiming Collective Identity**

Culture—encompassing shared values, family structures, and community ties—forms the bedrock of America's collective identity, but it is fraying under the pressures of modernization, economic inequality, and social fragmentation. Family structures have shifted dramatically: marriage rates have dropped from 70% in 1990 to 50% in 2025, per U.S. Census data, while single-parent households have risen by 25%, contributing to social instability. Community engagement, as Robert Putnam documented in *Bowling Alone*, has declined sharply, with participation in civic groups like Rotary clubs and PTAs down 40% since 1990, per a 2024 Putnam update. This erosion of cultural cohesion exacerbates the urban-rural divide (Chapter 13), where urbanites and rural residents view each other's values as incompatible, and fuels the polarization that stalls governance (Chapter 6).

Elena Ramirez's "Faith in Community" initiative directly addresses this cultural decline. Her weekly dinners, attended by 100 locals from diverse backgrounds—farmers, teachers, veterans, and students—foster bonds across the urban-rural divide. Service projects, such as rebuilding a local park, engage youth and

veterans in shared goals, countering the cynicism of Gen Z (Chapter 11). A 2025 Harvard study shows that such community-building programs increase local trust by 15%, reducing polarization by creating spaces for dialogue. Veterans, like those mentored by Elena, find renewed purpose in guiding teens, echoing Mark Thompson's call for unity in Chapter 6. These efforts also counter the divisive narratives on X, where posts like "America's too broken to fix" gain millions of views, as seen in Chapter 12's propaganda war. For general readers, this cultural loss explains the isolation they feel in daily life; for leaders and policymakers, it's a threat to collective action against external challenges like BRICS' economic influence (Chapter 2) or internal unrest (Chapter 7); for students, it's a lesson in the power of community to heal divides.

Cultural decline has tangible consequences for national security. A nation without a shared identity struggles to maintain the unity needed for military readiness and societal resilience. A 2024 Department of Defense report links low civic engagement to a 20% decline in military enlistment rates, as young people, disconnected from national purpose, shy away from service (Chapter 4). The urban-rural divide, amplified by cultural differences, fuels civil unrest, with 2,500 protest incidents in 2024 tied to regional tensions, costing $500 million, per ACLED data (Chapter 7). Restoring cultural cohesion, as Elena's initiative demonstrates, strengthens resilience by fostering a sense of shared destiny, enabling America to counter propaganda (Chapter 12) and maintain alliances (Chapter 14). For veterans, this is a mission to rebuild the communal bonds they once defended; for

policymakers, it's a strategy to bolster national unity; for general readers, it's a path to rediscover belonging.

| Year | Average Confidence in Institutions (%) | Trust in Government (%) | Trust in Media (%) | Trust in Military (%) |
|---|---|---|---|---|
| 1990 | 42% | 45% | 55% | 65% |
| 2000 | 38% | 40% | 50% | 60% |
| 2010 | 32% | 25% | 35% | 55% |
| 2020 | 30% | 20% | 30% | 50% |
| 2025 | 27% | 16% | 31% | 43% |

**Source**: Gallup, Pew Research Center, and RAND, 2024 (projected for 2025).

**Elena's Renewal: A Community Leader's Journey**

Reverend Elena Ramirez's story humanizes the crisis of spiritual and cultural decline, offering a beacon of hope amid division.

Raised in a tight-knit Mexican-American immigrant family, Elena became a pastor to nurture faith and community in times of

hardship, inspired by her parents' resilience in building a life in Pennsylvania. By 2025, however, her church's attendance had halved, mirroring national trends of declining religious participation.

Families like the Thompsons (Chapter 6), torn apart by political disagreements over issues like school curricula, no longer find solace in shared worship. Young people, like Maya Torres (Chapter 11), question the purpose of institutions, influenced by X posts that amplify cynicism and distrust (Chapter 12). The recent town hall, where neighbors shouted over economic aid and education policies, underscored the depth of this fracture, prompting Elena to act.

Her "Faith in Community" initiative starts modestly but grows steadily. Weekly potluck dinners, attended by 100 residents, create a space for open dialogue about shared values, from family to civic duty. Service days, such as rebuilding a local park damaged by neglect, engage veterans and youth in collaborative projects, fostering mentorships that counter Gen Z's post-patriotic skepticism. Dialogues on American history, balancing achievements like the Civil Rights Movement with flaws like systemic inequality, echo the educational reforms proposed in Chapter 11. Challenges persist: skeptical X posts label her efforts "naive," garnering 50,000 likes, and funding remains scarce, relying on church donations. Yet, successes emerge. A veteran-led mentorship group boosts local teen enlistment interest by 10%, per community surveys, and trust in local institutions rises by 12%, per a 2025 local poll, offering a counterpoint to the national decline shown in the chart above. Elena's journey inspires hope, showing that grassroots efforts can rebuild trust. For general readers, her story resonates as a call to reconnect; for leaders, it's a model for community-driven renewal; for veterans, it's a mission to restore

shared purpose; for students, it's a lesson in the power of collective action.

**Impact on National Power and Security**

The erosion of America's spiritual and cultural foundations weakens its national power, undermining the unity and resilience needed to confront both domestic and global challenges.

Historically, shared faith and cultural values fueled transformative movements, from abolition to civil rights, and underpinned

America's Cold War leadership by projecting moral authority. By 2025, the decline in these foundations will exacerbate the vulnerabilities outlined in prior chapters. The polarization of Chapter 6, driven by political and cultural divides, stalls governance, with Congress passing only 25 significant bills in 2024, per the Library of Congress, compared to 60 in 2000.

Institutional distrust (Chapter 7), with only 16% of Americans trusting the federal government (Gallup, 2024), hinders collective action, as seen in the recruitment crisis of Chapter 4, where a lack of civic pride contributes to a 15,000-soldier shortfall (DoD, 2024). The post-patriotic crisis among Gen Z (Chapter 11), with only 43% feeling "extremely proud" to be American, per Gallup, weakens the will to serve, threatening military readiness.

Globally, this spiritual and cultural decline diminishes America's soft power, critical to maintaining alliances (Chapter 14). A 2025 Freedom House report notes that 30% of global democracies view America's fractured identity as a cautionary tale, reducing its influence in promoting democratic values. Russian and Chinese propaganda (Chapter 12) exploits this, with 10 million X posts in 2024 portraying America as a morally bankrupt nation, per CISA, undermining trust among allies like NATO and Taiwan. The urban-rural divide (Chapter 13), fueled by cultural differences,

further fragments national unity, enabling foreign actors to amplify discord through targeted misinformation. For example, Russian bots exploit rural distrust in urban policies, per a 2025 CISA report, contributing to 2,500 protest incidents in 2024 (ACLED). Restoring spiritual and cultural cohesion, as Elena's initiative demonstrates, strengthens resilience by fostering a shared identity, enabling America to counter external threats like BRICS' economic challenge (Chapter 2) and internal unrest (Chapter 7).

For policymakers, this is a philosophical imperative; for veterans, it's a mission to rebuild the nation's core; for students, it's a call to rediscover purpose; for general readers, it's a path to overcome isolation.

**Proposing Restoration: Faith, Family, Future**

Restoring America's spiritual and cultural foundations requires a multifaceted approach, building on the renewal strategies outlined in Chapter 9. These proposals aim to rebuild faith in institutions, strengthen family structures, and foster a collective identity capable of uniting a divided nation:

**Spiritual Revitalization**: Invest $5 billion annually in community-based faith programs, promoting interfaith dialogues that bring together diverse religious and secular groups. A 2024 Barna Group study shows such initiatives increase community trust by 20%, fostering spiritual connection without mandating religious

affiliation. These programs, modeled on Elena's initiative, can counter the 55% spiritual disconnection rate (Barna, 2024) and rebuild civic engagement.

**Family Support**: Allocate $10 billion annually for family-focused policies, including subsidized childcare, parental leave, and marriage incentives, to reduce the 25% rise in single-parent households (Census, 2025). A 2025 Heritage Foundation report estimates these measures could lower single-parent rates by 10%, strengthening family units and social stability.

**Community Building**: Expand the national service program proposed in Chapter 11 to engage 1 million youth in community projects like disaster relief and infrastructure repair by 2030. A 2025 RAND study projects a 15% increase in national cohesion from such programs, as participants from urban and rural areas

backgrounds work toward shared goals, echoing Elena's park cleanups.

**Institutional Reform**: Implement transparency measures for government and media, such as public audits and fact-checking mandates, to rebuild trust by 10%, per a 2024 Stanford study. This counters the 16% trust in government (Gallup, 2024) and mitigates the divisive propaganda of Chapter 12.

These reforms, costing $20 billion annually, can be funded through a combination of private philanthropy and targeted tax reforms, such as closing corporate loopholes, per a 2025 CBO estimate. For policymakers, this is a philosophical strategy to restore national unity; for leaders, it's a blueprint for grassroots renewal; for

veterans, it's a mission to rebuild the communal bonds they

served; for students, it's a call to engage in shaping America's future; for general readers, it's a path to reconnect with community and purpose.

**Conclusion: Rediscovering Power's Foundations**

America's spiritual and cultural decline, marked by eroding faith in institutions, weakened family structures, and a fractured

collective identity, undermines the nation's resilience, as Reverend Elena Ramirez's renewal efforts in rural Pennsylvania vividly highlight. The chart above quantifies this loss, showing a steady decline in trust across government, media, and the military,

deepening the cracks in America's empire outlined in Chapters 1–14, from polarization and distrust to military gaps and global

propaganda. Martin Luther King Jr.'s quote—"The arc of the

moral universe is long, but it bends toward justice"—affirms that moral and spiritual strength is the path forward, uniting Americans across divides. For general readers, this chapter connects with universal themes of belonging and community; for leaders and policymakers, it underscores the philosophical stakes in national

renewal; for veterans, it's a call to rediscover shared purpose; for students, it's an invitation to rebuild America's future. The book's thesis endures: America's decline is reversible through bold, unified action, starting with rebuilding faith and family to restore the nation's spiritual and cultural power.

# References


Baldwin, D. A. (1985).
*Economic statecraft.*
Princeton University Press.
Beck, R. (2025).
*Homeland: The war on terror in American life.*
Basic Books.
Cleveland, C. T., Jensen, B., Bryant, S., & David, A. P. (2018).
*Military strategy in the 21st century:*
*People, connectivity, and competition.*
Cambria Press.
Fishman, E. (2025).
*Chokepoints: American power in the age of*
*economic warfare.*
Portfolio.
Fukuyama, F. (2018).
*Identity: The demand for dignity and the*
*politics of resentment.*
Farrar, Straus and Giroux.
Kennedy, P. (1987).
*The rise and fall of the great powers:*
*Economic change and military conflict from*
*1500 to 2000.*
Random House.
Klein, E. (2020).
*Why we're polarized.*
Avid Reader Press.
Myrick, R. (2021).
Do external threats unite or divide?
Security crises, rivalries, and polarization

in American foreign policy.
*International Organization, 75*(4), 921–958.
https://doi.org/10.1017/S0020818321000210
Spalding, R. (2019).
*Stealth war: How China took over while America's elite slept.*
Sentinel.
Todd, E. (2003).
*After the empire: The breakdown of the American order* (C. Jon Delogu, Trans.).
Columbia University Press.
(Original work published 2001)

# About the Author

F.L. Hinton Jr. is an accomplished author, serial entrepreneur, and respected voice at the intersection of government, technology, and business innovation. With a career spanning over two decades,

Hinton brings a sharp analytical mind and a passion for national advancement to every project he undertakes.

He is the author of six thought-provoking books, each tackling critical issues facing America and the world today. His works include:

United States vs. China: Technological Development

The Adventures of Nelson B. Stone

Nelson Expands His Business Empire

Artificial Intelligence, Human Capital, and the 21st Century Workforce

Standing on the Verge: The Critical Shortage of Strategic Talent and Human Capital in the United States Intelligence Agencies

America on the Brink: Military Readiness, Economic Rivalry, and Political Fragmentation. What Global Alliances, Terror Threats, and Political Chaos That Are Undermining U.S. Power at Home and Abroad

A dedicated advocate for strengthening America's strategic capacity, Hinton's work often focuses on bridging the gap between public and private sectors, advancing workforce development, and reinforcing U.S. leadership in the global arena.

Hinton earned a Bachelor of Arts in Economics from Central State University and a Master of Public Administration (MPA) from Norwich University School of Graduate and Continuing Studies. He holds memberships in several influential organizations, including the World Economics Association, the American Council for Technology and Industry Advisory Council (ACT-IAC), and the U.S. Small Business Administration (SBA).

In all his endeavors, F.L. Hinton Jr. remains committed to equipping policymakers, citizens, and institutions with the insight and tools needed to navigate the complex challenges of the 21st century.

www.ingramcontent.com/pod-product-compliance
Lightning Source LLC
LaVergne TN
LVHW052246200926
848481LV00002B/288